YOUR
PLAYBOOK
FOR
BEATING
DEPRESSION

Essential Strategies for Managing and Living with Depr

Cliff Rich~~ey and~~

Mary E. Garrison, LCSW, ACSW

Associate Professor of Social Work

YOUR PLAYBOOK FOR BEATING DEPRESSION

"Your Playbook for Beating Depression: Essential Strategies for Managing and Living with Depression" is published by New Chapter Press (www.NewChapterMedia.com) and distributed by the IPG (www.IPGBook.com) © Cliff Richey and Mary Garrison, 2017

ISBN: 978-1937559687

For more information on this title or New Chapter Press contact: Randy Walker, Managing Partner, New Chapter Press, 1175 York Ave, Suite #3s, New York, NY 10065 Rwalker@NewChapterMedia.com

Dedicated To Betty Richey

Loving mother to Cliff and his sister Nancy

A wonderful mother and lady, who will be missed

Table of Contents

About The Authors

Cliff Richey was known as the original "Bad Boy" of tennis before there was John McEnroe and Ilie Nastase. His career was highlighted by a 1970 season where he led the United States to the Davis Cup title, finished as the first-ever Grand Prix world points champion and won one of the most exciting matches in American tennis history that clinched the year-end No. 1 American ranking. He won both of his singles matches in the 5-0 U.S. victory over West Germany in the 1970 Davis Cup final, while he beat out rivals Rod Laver, Ken Rosewall, Arthur Ashe and Stan Smith to win the first-ever Grand Prix world points title the precursor to the modern day ATP rankings. At the 1970 Pacific Coast

Championships at the Berkeley Tennis Club in Berkeley, Calif., he earned the No. 1 U.S. ranking when he beat Smith in a fifth-set tie-breaker, where both players had simultaneous match point in a sudden-death nine-point tie-breaker at 4-4. He also reached the semifinals of both the 1970 French and U.S. Opens, losing a famous match to Zeljko Franulovic of Yugoslavia in the French semifinals, despite holding match points and leading by two-sets-to-one and 5-1 in the fourth set. He also reached the semifinals again at the U.S. Open in 1972, losing to Arthur Ashe, and reached the quarterfinals of Wimbledon in 1971, losing to Ken Rosewall. Richey won 45 career singles titles and with his sister Nancy Richey, a singles champion at the French and Australian championships, is the best brother-sister combination ever in American tennis.

While Richey was known for his tantrums and boorish behavior during his career, his actions served simply as a mask for his internal struggle with clinical depression. During his darkest days, Richey would place black trash bags over the windows of his house, stay in bed all day and cry. With the same determination that earned him the nick-name "The Bull," Richey fought against his depression that was not diagnosed until just before his 50th birthday during a routine visit to the skin doctor. Since his happenstance diagnosis, Richey has steadily been taking the anti-depressant drug Zoloft that has greatly improved his quality of life and moved him to become an advocate for mental health, speaking at numerous events and gatherings across the country. He is now a mental health advocate and authored the book "Acing Depression: A Tennis Champion's Toughest Match," published in 2010 by New Chapter Press. He also gives speeches, presentations and talks around the country and provides hope to people with the crippling disease of depression. Cliff can be reached at Cliff.Richey@yahoo.com.

Mary E. Garrison (MSW, University of Illinois at Urbana-Champaign; LCSW; ACSW), is an Associate Professor of Social Work at Millikin University. Mary has had extensive practice experience in the social work field, with many years of practice in the mental health field. Throughout her career, Mary has served as a therapist, clinical supervisor, manager, clinical consultant, and advocate. Mary has been active in providing continuing education opportunities for colleagues through professional workshops, presentations, and trainings both domestically and internationally. Mary serves as advisor to multiple committees, is a member of the Governing Board of the Macon County Continuum of Care and serves as the Point-in-Time Homeless Count Coordinator for Macon County. Mary is a statewide National

Association of Social Workers Illinois (NASW IL) Awards Committee Member, Delegate Assembly Member, and has previously served as the East Central District Nomination Committee Chair and immediate past chair of the East Central District and Member-at-Large for NASW IL. Mary has been an active member of NAMI Illinois sitting on the Board of Directors and Legislative Committee. Mary is a past recipient of the NASW Illinois Social Worker of the Year Award, the Cesar Chavez Social Justice Award and the first ever Macon County Continuum of Care Advocate of the Year Award in 2015. If you are interested in having Mary speak at an event or for consultation, you may contact her at mgarrison@millikin.edu or 217-424-5074.

DISCLAIMER

The information and solutions offered in this book are intended to serve as guidelines for managing mental health issues. Please discuss specific symptoms and medical conditions with your doctor.

From The Authors

Our Personal and Professional journey

After my book *Acing Depression: A Tennis Champion's Toughest Match* was published I have been asked if I was going to do another book. My answer was always the same, "Only if I felt another book could help the many who suffer the disease I know so well – clinical depression." My first book told my story of battling depression. I have been in good recovery for 20 years and I wanted people to know that no matter how deep the depression is, there is hope for a good future. Hope is the word and feeling that clinical depression tries to take from us. But, there is hope. There is hope.

I approached my recovery from clinical depression as a tough opponent across the net.

I was in a battle. I truly had a very rough match facing me and always had to be the captain of my "team." Tennis is such an individual sport yet I always had a good support group on the world tennis tour with coaches, practice partners, mentors and sponsors. I absorbed their knowledge and then go do battle against the toughest pros in the world. That training I put to use to compete against probably my toughest foe – clinical depression – and I am winning. There is recovery. There is hope. *Your Playbook for Beating Depression* can help you be the captain and your team and win the match against depression.

My co-author Mary Garrison is a great friend whom I met in October of 2010. We were both speakers at the Montana State National Alliance on Mental Illness (NAMI) Conference. We met the first day at breakfast and for the next three days we shared our respective stories of becoming mental health advocates. We stayed in touch and the following May, Mary invited me to speak at her institution, Millikin University in Decatur, Illinois where she is an Associate Professor of Social Work.

Over the last few years I have thought about doing a book that tries to answer the questions I hear as I travel the country and speak at many events. "I think I have depression and what do I do about it?" With Mary Garrison's training and expertise and my first-hand experience with the disease, I asked Mary to join me in writing this book. We are sort of the "coach and the player." Let me digress and say this to those who are suffering and reading this book right now. Neither Mary nor I have a "magic wand" we can use to heal you. But, having been flat on my back with clinical depression for three long years, I can confidently tell you there is life after depression. I want you to believe there is hope.

Like other diseases, medical research has offered new and proven therapies that can be used and are effective.

I told Mary I wanted to write a book that was a "first aid kit" for those who suffer and we hope *Your Playbook for Beating Depression* is that book. Thank you, Mary, for being my co-author.

– Cliff Richey

Let me create a picture for you………... Billings, Montana, October 27, 2010. It is 7 am and I am at the top floor restaurant of a hotel where I am staying as I have been invited to be a keynote speaker for the Montana State NAMI Conference. I strategically positioned myself to be hidden in the corner reviewing my notes for "the big show" at 9 am. I notice a few others in the restaurant as I nervously look around and then focus again on my notes. As I nibble on my breakfast and devour my first (of many) diet cokes of the day, a gentleman approaches, "Hello Mary, I am Cliff Richey." Immediately I look up and think…who knows me in Billings, Montana? I don't know who Cliff Richey is. I am an unknown entity and perplexed by this gentleman's familiarity with me.

"Hello and good morning, nice to meet you Cliff," I said.

"I just wanted to say hi and wish you well today. I will leave you alone to prepare and see you later," Cliff said.

"Thank you Cliff. I appreciate your well wishes and I will see you later today."

That exchange was the start of a wonderful friendship.

Cliff attended my opening keynote address and I attended his address as well. During the next three days, all our time in between sessions, lunches and dinners were spent talking about mental illness, recovery and getting to know one another – three days that changed our lives for the better. As I left Montana, I told Cliff I would see him again and that I wanted him to come present at the university where I teach. Fast forward to the following May when Cliff visited Decatur and Millikin University to celebrate *May is Mental Health Month*. Cliff and I remained in touch and I was honored when he asked me to partner with him as a co-author on this book.

This project has been a journey that has forced me to be challenged, experience risk, continue growing and engage in reflection on my abilities, commitments and purpose. I am a social worker with passion, drive and a commitment to social justice and advocacy and believe that everyone has a right to experience the best possible life they can. In my work I hope I have been able to make a difference and improve people's lives. Thank you Cliff for allowing me to be on this journey with you – I am honored and humbled.

– Mary E. Garrison, LCSW, ACSW
Associate Professor of Social Work

Foreword

Dusty McCoy, Executive Director of West Texas Counseling & Guidance

Cliff Richey and Mary Garrison have been champions for mental health treatment for many years, working tirelessly to breakdown the stigma that surrounds access and receiving treatment for mental health. Cliff's courage to speak out about his battle with depression has helped encourage others to seek treatment and these conversations surrounding behavioral health, and in particular personal, intimate stories of one's experiences are of the utmost importance across our country. As evidenced in Cliff Richey's home town of San Angelo, TX, depression and suicide rates are at an unacceptable level and unfortunately very common across our nation. Two hundred and thirty-three people have died by suicide in

Cliff's home town from 2000 to 2014. Through education and awareness, great strides have been made in the acceptance of mental health treatment, but we have a long way to go and cannot view the work thus far to be enough, we must continue to fight for treatment access and the reduction of stigma.

Stigma plays a significant part in many individuals decision to not seek treatment. Keeping one's mental health symptoms a secret and feeling they just need to "take care of it on their own" is a common theme due to fear of weakness, judgment and discrimination as a result of stigma. One's lack of seeking treatment for a treatable condition is not a sign of strength and only exacerbates the condition leading to a more critical health state. We would never attribute lack of treatment for any other medical issue as a sign of strength. Not only should we be open for ourselves to seek treatment; we should encourage others to do so as well. Recently, Bruce Springsteen joined the conversation by publicly discussing his battle of depression, and, like Cliff Richey, his relief came through antidepressants and psychotherapy. So many times, the first time a friend or loved one begins the therapeutic process it was from someone's personal story of a direct experience with depression and anxicty.

What can we do to help people break the stigma of receiving mental health treatment and gaining access to treatment? It may seem overwhelming and complicated, but first and foremost ongoing, consistent advocacy for additional funding initiatives for mental health and support of local nonprofit mental health providers is essential. There is no doubt that access to quality mental health services is a crisis facing our entire nation and especially our rural communities. Collaborative care with primary care providers and the use of technology such as psychiatric telemedicine programs provides hope for the future of behavioral health care.

To breakdown the stigma that surrounds mental health conditions, join the conversation and do your part…educate anyone and everyone about mental health conditions, share your story, and support those you know who are facing a diagnosis letting them know that recovery CAN happen. When quality mental health resources are available for depression, they are useless if the person suffering is not willing to access them.

My hope is that through the efforts of this book, Cliff and Mary's work, and the many mental health advocates across our country, we can see an increase of individuals seeking treatment, a transformation of our nation's mental health system and begin to see treatment for behavioral health conditions and physical health conditions with equality.

This book is a fantastic resource and serves as a starting point for the creation of your team and your journey of recovery to manage and live with your diagnosis of depression. As the journey begins, remember the old Chinese proverb, "tho journey of 100,000 miles begins with one step" and often times that first step is the toughest. Hopefully, "Your Playbook for Beating Depression" will make that first step less daunting.

Chapter 1

Depression: A Bully And A Liar

Bully: a blustering browbeating person; especially one habitually cruel to others who are weaker.

Liar: a person who tells lies.

-Merriam-Webster Dictionary (2015)

"Depression is a bully. A kid who picks on you when you're weak. But if you stand up to him, he'll back off pretty quick. Sometimes he'll put up a fight, but bullies are not strong men, necessarily. They aren't as rough and tumble as they want you to think. If you stand up to it, clinical depression will also back down."

—*Cliff Richey, Acing Depression*

A perspective from Cliff:

I am pretty opinionated on things I know from experience. I tell people all the time there are two things I know really well...tennis and clinical depression. I have lived both of them and both are definitely a part of who I am. In my life, they have a relationship to one another.

My dad was a pro tennis player and my sister Nancy was as well. I followed their path and, at 12 years old, knew and wanted to be a successful pro tennis player. I knew from their example I had to work hard and give 100 percent to attain the needed skill. Skill is, and has been, the key word in my life and career. I want to win and be the last guy standing at the end of the tournament and skill would get me there. I discovered early on that it was fun to feel improvement and to feel your skills getting better the harder the work. You could easily say I was "hooked" on developing my skill.

From age 12 to 45, I had the success I dreamed of, I played junior tennis, the pro tour and the senior pro tour. In my 30-year career, I played 500 events all over the world and over 1,500 matches, becoming the best in each division I entered. Skill got me there.

I started drinking a few beers to relax and be "part of the locker room" at 17 or 18 years old. I also took some valium at times to help me sleep and cope with the challenge of jet lag. My skills were good. I was winning. I would have a few beers to celebrate and if the odd hours were a problem, I'd pop a valium to sleep better and all was well. It worked great until it didn't!

My best shot in tennis started to leave me. My backhand became a cracking shot and not the reliable stroke it had always been. I was 25 years old at the time, just about the average age for onset of clinical depression. That was 1972 and I played six more years on the world tour and it became a living hell. A beer to celebrate became beers to drown the pain. My sleep became more erratic and the valium intake increased so I could sleep better, so I thought. My skills kept slipping and my career was on the downward slope. I had clinical depression. I know that now but I did not know that then.

My grandfather had depression and that is probably the genetic link to me. I have learned that big losses and stressors in life can trigger clinical depression. For me at age 25, loss of my skill was catastrophic. There was a perfect storm...I knew things were not right but I could not pinpoint what. It would be almost 25 years before I got diagnosed and into effective treatment.

Depression is a bully and a liar. Bully's come at you when you are in a weakened state and are vulnerable. Depression is a liar because it tries to make you feel that all hope is gone. My 'team" was made up of many players, my coaches, sparring partners, trainers and good doctors that helped me reach the top of pro tennis. You can build a team to compete and win in tennis and

against the overwhelming foe of clinical depression. Let me tell you...there is hope, there is recovery...there is life beyond depression.

The term depression has shifted from a taboo word to a more mainstream, common, causal word with virtually everyone in this day and age familiar with it in some way. Many routinely use the term depression to describe feeling "blue," "sad" and "down" yet lack a true understanding of what depression really means. Depression *IS* a bully and a liar as the symptoms one experiences with the illness are confusing, misleading and incongruent with how we normally feel and want to understand the illness. Phrases such as "snap out of it" and "you're just sad" suggests that a person who is depressed has the ability to just take charge and change their mood and have control over the symptoms at their will – as if it is a choice to be depressed or not.

Depression has incredible strength and power that is misunderstood by many and intimidating for individuals' suffering from it to believe they can "get over it." Many would argue that we have come a long way in terms of our acceptance of the word depression as a way to define that we are down, having a bad day or just are not feeling right. We continue to lack a full and accurate understanding of depression as a clinical illness and the significant impact it has and leaves on individuals, families, friends and society as a whole.

Prevalence of Depression

Prevalence of mental illness as a whole is very common in the United States, "approximately one in five adults in the U.S., 43.7 million, or 18.6 percent, experiences mental illness in a given year," according to NAMI in 2016. Mental illness does not discriminate with regard to age, race, socioeconomic class or gender and leaves individuals who are diagnosed with mental illness a difficult path to navigate in life if they are not armed with a playbook to beat this very fierce opponent. Focusing specifically on depression, the numbers are also staggering in terms of who is affected. According to NAMI, "an estimated 16 million American adults - almost 7 percent of the population - had at least one major depressive episode last year." Similar to all mental health issues, individuals of all ages and backgrounds (socioeconomic, racial, and ethnic) may experience depression, yet research tells us that some groups of individuals are affected at higher rates than others. Specifically, "women are 70 percent more likely than men to experience depression, and young adults aged 18–25 are 60 percent more likely to have depression than people age 50 or older." Another powerful statistic from NAMI is that "depression is the leading cause of disability worldwide, and is a major contributor to the global burden of disease" resulting in critically high costs to individuals on multiple levels including emotionally, financially and relationally. Depression and many other mental illnesses are often left untreated leading to significant consequences for individuals, families and communities. According to NAMI mental health facts, almost 60 percent of adults and 50 percent of youth ages 8-15 did not receive mental health treatment in the previous year. According to National Institute of Health (NIH), depression causes a significant loss to employers due to lack of productivity. Further, NIH indicates that untreated mental illness results in losses to schools and overall educational systems due to children's inability to focus and get the necessary and appropriate supports. Lack of treatment also impacts individuals, families and peers leading to long term negative impact for all.

Depression is everywhere and my guess is if we are not ourselves dealing with depression, we know someone who is...a family member, peer, friend, or co-worker. Mental illness is a public health issue that lacks appropriate attention due to the absence of education, stigma and fear. We _MUST_ begin to take a stand and provide the advocacy, support and resources necessary to hit these staggering statistics head on and decrease the risk for all while offering options and hope to individuals diagnosed with mental illness. It is difficult for individuals to admit they have clinical depression due to the stigma our society places on mental illness.

Understanding mental illness from a physical illness perspective is imperative. The brain is a part of our body and we need to treat mental illness just as we need to treat physical illnesses. For some reason our society is willing to accept when individuals are diagnosed with the flu, diabetes, heart conditions and cancer, yet society is unwilling to equate a mental illness, such as clinical depression, to a physical illness. The World Health Organization (WHO) defines health as "a state of complete physical, mental and social well-being and not merely the absence of disease or infirmity." Policy links mental and physical illness together but humans have created this false belief that mental illness is not part of our overall health, leading to lack of treatment as individuals often feel they have to figure out what is going on themselves instead of seeking treatment as they would for any physical illness such as cancer or diabetes.

Understanding Clinical Depression

To gain a comprehensive understanding of clinical depression, defining the term depression as well as the symptoms becomes crucial. Depression is defined by Mayo Clinic as "a mood disorder that causes a persistent feeling of sadness and loss of interest." Major Depressive Disorder is the most current and accurate diagnostic term from the Diagnostic and Statistical Manual (DSM) 5, the standard for classifications of mental disorders utilized by mental health professionals to diagnose mental illnesses.

Major Depressive Disorder is also commonly called major depression or clinical depression and the American Psychiatric

Association (APA) states that it "is a medical illness that affects how you feel, think and behave causing persistent feelings of sadness and loss of interest in previously enjoyed activities." NAMI states that "depression is more than just feeling sad or going through a rough patch, it's a serious mental health condition that requires understanding, treatment and a good recovery plan." Lastly, the National Institute of Mental Health (NIMH) defines major depression as "severe symptoms that interfere with your ability to work, sleep, study, eat, and enjoy life. An episode can occur only once in a person's lifetime, but more often, a person has several episodes."

Symptoms of Depression

There are common symptoms that are often present with individuals experiencing depression. Although each person experiences symptoms in different ways, there are common symptoms that negatively impact one's ability to function in one's typical day-to-day routine. The National Collaborating Centre for Mental Health says that individuals may experience symptoms related to changes in sleep, appetite and movement, lack of concentration and interest, loss of energy, low self-esteem, hopelessness and overall physical body "aches and pains" with no clear cause.

The disease of depression is complex and difficult to truly understand the particular causes of the illness. Pinpointing one's cause for depression can be arduous as there is no one single cause. Harvard Health Publication states that "it's often said that depression results from a chemical imbalance, but that figure of speech doesn't capture how complex the disease is." Research suggests that depression doesn't spring from simply having too much or too little of certain brain chemicals. Depression can be activated by experiencing critical life events, illness or other risk areas, or it may appear spontaneously without association to these aspects. Research has identified several specific factors that do contribute to the cause of depression including traumatic experiences, genetic influences, life situations and environmental circumstances, brain structure, chemicals and hormones, various medical conditions as well as substance abuse may all be contributors to the cause of one's depression.

Diagnosing depression may be more difficult than one would expect. For a clinical diagnosis of Major Depressive Disorder (also known as major or clinical depression), professionals identify specific symptoms based on diagnostic criterion that persists for a specific duration of time. NAMI provides a quick reference for the criteria of Major Depression:

A person must have experienced a major depressive episode that has lasted longer than two weeks. The symptoms of a major depressive episode include:

- Loss of interest or loss of pleasure in all activities

- Change in appetite or weight

- Sleep disturbances

- Feeling agitated or feeling slowed down

- Fatigue

- Feelings of low self-worth, guilt or shortcomings

- Difficulty concentrating or making decisions

- Suicidal thoughts or intentions

You can go to NAMI.org to read more about symptoms and DSM 5 criteria for Major

Depressive Disorder. If you are experiencing any of these symptoms, it is suggested that you seek out medical care by either a primary care physician or better yet, a specialized physician who is knowledgeable about mental illness as soon as possible. Whether you "meet the criteria" for a clinical diagnosis of Major Depressive Disorder or not, you can learn more and receive treatment for your symptoms as you do not have to continue to live with these difficult symptoms. Treatment is available.

Why is a clinical diagnosis important for a person to have when they are facing depression? Just as with any physical illness, a mental illness is a medical condition and obtaining a clinical diagnosis for your mental illness will first and foremost provide you a foundation from which to start with a name and some answers for what you are experiencing. Often times, individuals find it hard to communicate how they are feeling and experience a lack of empathy and support from others as they are just told to "get over it." A clinical diagnosis provides one with the confirmation and validation that they are experiencing an illness just as if you had a physical illness; mental illness is equivalent to physical illness. Once you know "what you have" you can begin to talk about treatment options and learn how to manage your illness, understand the prognosis and identify the necessary treatment providers and specialists you will need to recruit for your team. Having a diagnosis is often difficult to hear, yet can bring comfort and direction regarding how one will need to proceed.

Suicide and Depression

Suicide is a significant concern for individuals with mental illness. According to NAMI, 90 percent of those who die by suicide experience a mental illness. Often the mental illness is undiagnosed or untreated. Experiencing mental illness is the top risk factor for suicide. Further, suicide is a risk factor for individuals with clinical (major) depression leaving many people at risk for harm. The severity of symptoms for some individuals experiencing depression contributes to a loss of hope and often leads to the emergence of suicidal thoughts and behaviors.

"I don't want to do this anymore."

"If I just disappeared, everyone would be better off."

"I'll relieve every one of the burden of me."

"I'm ready to die."

"I am going to kill myself."

Without a doubt, these words are difficult to hear, and maybe you've even had these thoughts. You wouldn't be alone. Suicidal thinking is a common side effect of the mental health diagnosis of depression. Unfortunately, far too many people in the United States have lost their battle to depression and have taken their lives by completing suicide, leaving loved ones behind with devastating effects.

Who's at risk? According to the National Institute of Mental Health, the risk factors for suicide include: depression, other mental disorders, substance abuse, a prior suicide attempt, family history of mental disorders or substance abuse, family history of suicide, family violence, having firearms in the home, incarceration and being exposed to the suicidal behavior of others. Further, the NIMH states that men are more likely to die by suicide than women, but women are more likely to attempt suicide. According to the American Foundation for Suicide Prevention (AFSP) seven out of ten suicides are by white males. Suicide is the 10th leading cause of death, with more people dying by suicide than homicide. White males over 65 are most likely to die by suicide. Not surprisingly, men are less likely than women to seek mental health treatment. Why is this? Although much progress has been made in the area of changing the stigma of mental illness, the stigma still exists, and likely more so for men than women. Women tend to be more open to seeking treatment for health problems in general, and mental health problems seem to be included. Males are more prone to believing ideas such as "real men don't talk about their problems" and "if I seek mental health treatment, I'm weak." These kinds of beliefs will greatly help or hinder a person's willingness to reach out for help.

It is essential that you and your team know the *warning signs* of suicide and risk factors that are involved in order to provide support and protection for yourself, your family member or friend who is experiencing difficulties. Warning signs from the National Alliance on Mental Illness include:

- Threats or comments about killing themselves, also known as suicidal ideation, can begin with seemingly harmless thoughts like "I wish I wasn't here" but can become more overt and dangerous

- Increased alcohol and drug use

- Aggressive behavior. A person who's feeling suicidal may experience higher levels of aggression and rage than they are used to

- Social withdrawal from friends, family and the community

- Dramatic mood swings indicate that your loved one is not feeling stable and may feel suicidal

- Preoccupation with talking, writing or thinking about death

- Impulsive or reckless behavior

Suicide is a complicated and confusing issue. When trying to understand how a person gets to the place of considering or completing suicide, it may be helpful to consider a theoretical approach. One such theoretical approach, Crisis Theory, is presented by Dr. Frank Campbell. His theory suggests that a crisis is a time-limited phase where the emotions of a person reacting to life pressures have broken down normal coping mechanisms. Stressors such as relationship difficulties, employment, legal and financial issues can create a hazardous atmosphere making us more susceptible to a full-blown crisis. The old adage "the straw that broke the camel's back" helps us understand how stressors can lead to suicide. Instead of straw, Campbell refers to these stressors as bricks. Stressors begin to pile up and coping begins to break down. Signs of ineffective coping include withdrawing from our supportive community; losing control over our physical well-being and daily activities as well as losing the sense of having a productive and creative life. These stressors or "bricks" begin to pile up until one becomes the tipping point which becomes the precipitating event – or PE - that leads to a full blown crisis. This full blown crisis can lead to suicide ambivalence.

At this point, the person wrestles between life and death. Thoughts of hopelessness and the sense of being a burden to others move the person closer to suicide. When this occurs, the person believes that there is no chance that life can get better and their loved ones would be better off without them. As long as the person continues to talk, there is hope. When the person quits talking, a decision is made and suicide is imminent. *If you find yourself in this place, it is time to reach out to a mental health professional and let them assist you with a safety plan.*

It is essential that while reaching out for help, you also think about reasons to live. Dr. Monica Basco suggests making a list of reasons to live by asking yourself these questions:

- Why shouldn't I leave?

- Who are the people to live for?

- What are the things I would miss?

- What experiences have I not had?

- What are the things that matter to me?

According to Basco, creating and reviewing this list can be beneficial and help us make it through the day and to the next. Although this is helpful to many, some people are in such a dark place that they can't come up with reasons to live. Hopelessness is the top indicator of suicide and therefore we need to look for reasons to have hope. (See appendix A for a worksheet on *Reasons to Live* to assist you in making this list.)

Making a list of reasons for hope can be very valuable as well. When looking for reasons for hope, resist the urge to tell yourself that there is no hope so why bother. Basco provides a list of questions that can be helpful. Answer all of the questions below, even if some do not pertain to your current situation:

- Are you doing anything differently now that might suggest there is hope for improvement?

  ◦ Many times the answer is, "yes, I'm in counseling, I started a new medicine, I joined the gym, I reached out to a friend."

- Are the problems that bring you down likely temporary? Will they resolve themselves with time?

  ○ Sometimes our problems are permanent such as in the case of grief and loss but other times they are not. Often times when we look back on our problems after months or years we can see the good that has come from challenge that our problem created and couldn't imagine our lives any other way.

- Why do other people believe that there is hope for the future?

  ○ People often ask, "Does this question pertain to other's perspective about themselves or their perspective about me?" Ask yourself both, why do people believe that there is hope for theirs and yours.

- Is it possible that you have not yet given it all of your effort?

  ◦ Most of the time people answer this question with a resounding "no."

- Have you been through times like these before?

  ◦ Have things usually gotten better with time, effort and patience? Most people have been through many hardships in a lifetime and sometimes past events have been much tougher than the current event that has led to the crisis. Most would agree that is true that things have gotten much better with time, patience and effort.

Once you have answered all of the questions, come to a conclusion incorporating all of the answers on one statement and write it down on an index card. Refer back to this card frequently, reminding yourself of why there is hope. (See appendix B for a worksheet on *Reasons to Have Hope* to assist you in answering these questions.)

What can one do to help others who may experience thoughts of suicide? A common myth is that by asking someone if they are having thoughts of suicide, they become more likely to die by suicide. This is simply not true. We need more nosey people, friends and neighbors who are not afraid to ask the question, "Are you thinking of hurting yourself?" Although this may be awkward, a simple but direct question could save a life. Pay attention to changes in your loved ones and listen closely.

When friends and family have become disengaged in life, be nosey. If you know that someone is going through a tough time, ask them probing, direct questions. If they report that they are in fact suicidal, take the statement seriously and act on it. Never dismiss a statement about possible self-harm as not being serious. If the person is not willing to get help, you may have to call law enforcement to intervene and force a mental health screening. Many times people are reluctant to intervene due to a sense of overstepping boundaries. Remember, this is a life and death situation. Embarrassing ourselves or someone else, possibly ruining a relationship, or making someone angry are not good reasons to not intervene. The person may, in fact, have a response different than you expect. They could be grateful, thankful, and relieved. You may be the only person who steps up to ask. Be that person. You may save a life.

Substance Use / Abuse and Mental Illness – Co-occurring Conditions

The connection of substance use and mental illness is extremely common. According to NAMI, scientific studies suggesting nearly "one-third of all people experiencing mental illnesses and about one-half of people living with severe mental illnesses (including bipolar disorder and schizophrenia) also experience substance abuse." Conversely, "these statistics are mirrored in the substance abuse community, where more than one-third of all alcohol abusers and more than one-half of all drug abusers report experiencing a mental illness."

This common connection is referred to as what is called co-occurring conditions (formally referred to as dual diagnosis) where individuals experience substance abuse or dependence and a mental illness that results in complex and difficult management of mental health issues. According to NAMI, "this is unfortunately a common situation - many people with mental illness have ongoing substance abuse problems, and many people who abuse drugs and alcohol also experience mental illness."

The Substance Abuse and Mental Health Services Administration (SAMHSA) is a department within the U.S. Department of Health and Human Services and focuses on awareness, education and ensuring effective and accessible treatment for individuals facing mental illness and substance abuse. According to SAMHSA, there is a strong correlation between depression and substance abuse with severe consequences, "approximately 8.9 million adults have co-occurring disorders...only 7.4 percent of individuals receive treatment for both conditions with 55.8 percent receiving no treatment at all".

Why do individuals who experience mental illness use substances? Often times individuals are not aware that they have a diagnosable mental illness, they are experiencing "something" (what are learned later by the individual to be symptoms) and turn to substances to "self-medicate" as the drugs and alcohol can momentarily feel good and seemingly relieve these feelings. The term *self-medicate* refers to the "the use of mood-altering substances, such as alcohol or opiates, in an attempt to alleviate depression, anxiety, or other psychiatric disorders," as described by the American Heritage Dictionary.

An article entitled *The Connection Between Mental Illness and Substance Abuse* from DualDiagnosis.org provides some examples of what self-medicating might look like; examples include "the depressed patient who uses marijuana to numb the pain, the patient suffering from social anxiety who drinks to feel more comfortable in social situations, the patient who struggles with panic attacks and takes benzodiazepines like Xanax or Valium in order to calm the symptoms or stop the attacks before they start, and the patient with low energy and lack of motivation who takes Adderall, cocaine or crystal meth to increase their drive to get things done."

Unfortunately, substance use actually exacerbates mental health issues and masks symptoms and causes challenges for individuals that are life altering and difficult to move beyond. When substance abuse is combined with mental illness, the prognosis for recovery is compromised and often very poor. Substance abuse can also cause symptom onset of an underlying mental illness that an individual may not be aware they have.

According to NAMI, "abuse of drugs and alcohol always results in a worse prognosis for a person with mental illness. Active users are less likely to follow through with their treatment plans. They are more likely to experience severe medical complications and early death. People with dual diagnosis are also at increased risk for impulsive and violent acts. Those who abuse drugs and alcohol are more likely to both attempt suicide and to die from their suicide attempts."

Treatment for co-occurring conditions can be difficult to access since historically treatment for mental illness and treatment for substance abuse were two very different arenas. According to SAMHSA, "integrated treatment works. Integrated treatment or treatment that addresses mental and substance use conditions at the same time is associated with lower costs and better outcomes such as reduced substance use, improved psychiatric symptoms and functioning, decreased hospitalization, increased housing stability, fewer arrests and improved quality of life." Integration occurs in several ways including programs offered as well as individual treatment with a therapist with a range of services and activities. Today, more options exist for the treatment of both disorders at the same time; simultaneously treating an individual's mental illness and their substance abuse disorder is imperative for a positive recovery journey.

Stigma and Mental Illness

"Ask for help when you need it. As we say in the locker room, 'Always have a game plan.' Stigma is an opponent too. Let us all reach out. We will beat stigma..."

- Cliff Richey,
San Angelo Standard Times, *2014*

According to an article from 2002 in *World Psychiatry* written by Patrick Corrigan and Amy Watson, "many people with serious mental illness are challenged doubly. On one hand, they struggle with the symptoms and disabilities that result from the disease. On the other, they are challenged by the stereotypes and prejudice that result from misconceptions about mental illness. As a result of both, people with mental illness are robbed of the opportunities that define a quality life: good jobs, safe housing, satisfactory health care, and affiliation with a diverse group of people." One in five adults in the U.S. - 43.8 million - experiences a mental illness in a given year and society as a whole continues to place judgment on and stigmatizes these individuals creating another unnecessary barrier to treatment and recovery. Stigma must be eliminated to accomplish these efforts; it is important to gain a clear understanding of stigma and the pervasive impact it has on individuals.

There are many definitions of stigma that exist. Here are several to provide an integrated perspective and understanding regarding the depth of impact stigma has:

- According to Bruce Link and Jo Phelan in the article "Conceptualizing Stigma" in the 2001 Annual Review of Sociology, stigma is "the co-occurrence of labeling, stereotyping, separation, status loss, and discrimination in a situation in which power is exercised."

- "Stigma is a mark of shame or discredit" (Merriam-Webster Dictionary, 2015).

- NAMI defines stigma as "an attempt to label a particular group of people as less worthy of respect than others, a mark of shame, disgrace or disapproval that results in discrimination."

- According to Kristalyn Salters-Pedneault in the "What is Stigma?" on HealthyPlace.com, stigma is "a perceived negative attribute that causes someone to devalue or think less of the whole person…anyone can see that stigma, of any kind, is a deeply negative mindset and provides no value to society in general."

In the words of NAMI, stigma is "not just a matter of using the wrong word or action – it's about disrespect." The impact of stigma is evident when you see words such as "shame" and "discredit" and "devalue" offering no value to society and individuals impacted by mental illness specifically.

In a 2002 article *"Understanding The Impact of Stigma on People with Mental Illness"* Corrigan and Watson of the University of Chicago Center for Psychiatric Rehabilitation and Consortium for Stigma Research assert that individuals who experience mental illness face dual challenges. First, they face the struggle that comes along with having a mental illness, the symptoms, residual effects and disabilities that are a consequence of the disease. Second and almost simultaneously, they face the stereotypes and prejudice – stigma – that come from the grave erroneous beliefs that society has regarding mental illness. These circumstances result in people with mental illness being deprived of the opportunities for a life they choose to lead. It impacts individual's chances with regard to quality of jobs, housing, health care, relationships and memberships with groups and people with which they choose to associate. There is still "much work that needs to be done to fully understand the breadth and scope of prejudice against people with mental illness."

Presently, the issue and impact of stigma has many public forums by which education and advocacy are working to change society's views, albeit the change is very slow. Society continues to struggle with understanding mental illness as a health / medical issue and therefore stigma raises its ugly head and people engage in public stigma and self-stigma - seeing persons with mental illness as just that, their illness, and not as an individual facing a health concern. Corrigan and Watson facilitate an understanding of public and self-stigma by defining and discussing both. "Public stigma is the reaction that the general population has to people with mental illness," wrote Corrigan and Watson. "Self-stigma is the prejudice which people with mental illness turn against themselves. Both public and self-stigma may be understood in terms of three components: stereotypes, prejudice, and discrimination." The table below depicts public and self-stigma with a comparison and contrast of the definitions:

Table 1 Comparing and contrasting the definitions of public stigma and self-stigma

---

Public stigma
Stereotype: Negative belief about a group (e.g., dangerousness, incompetence, character weakness)
Prejudice: Agreement with belief and/or negative emotional reaction (e.g., anger, fear)
Discrimination: Behavior response to prejudice (e.g., avoidance, withhold employment and housing opportunities, withhold help)

Self-stigma
Stereotype: Negative belief about the self (e.g., character weakness, incompetence)
Prejudice: Agreement with belief, negative emotional reaction (e.g., low self-esteem, low self-efficacy)
Discrimination: Behavior response to prejudice (e.g., fails to pursue work and housing opportunities)

-copied/adapted from: World Psychiatry, 2002, Feb 1(1), p 16-20, Patrick Corrigan and Amy Watson: *Forum – stigma and mental illness: Understanding the impact of stigma on people with mental illness.*

Moving from denial to acceptance

Denial of one's mental illness is the main barrier keeping individuals from becoming healthy and having opportunities available to them. Why would one deny a mental illness? Stigma! Society's view of mental illness creates a perfect excuse for individuals experiencing symptoms of mental illness to deny their illness. Although individuals experience symptoms from their developing illness and psychosocial dysfunction, stigma keeps them from accepting and taking action to challenge the illness. Acceptance is an action that creates vulnerability and opportunity for judgment from others yet it is the single most important part of moving forward in getting treatment, starting recovery and living a full and productive life with mental illness.

"We ain't doin' all this stuff the right way. Yes, both of these diseases (depression and Melanoma) kill but only one of them has a higher mortality rate that has nothing to do with the disease! Stigma! Stigma of mental illness is killing many people. Obviously no one person is at fault. But our community can do better."

- Cliff Richey,
San Angelo Standard Times, *2014*

Chapter 1 "Scorecard"
(Ways to know more)

Below are some topics to consider asking yourself (or your family member or friend) to see if help and support is necessary. If you answer yes to any of the statements below, please know you are not alone and helps is available now. Please contact your medical provider immediately. If you do not have a medical provider, please contact your local mental health center by searching the internet for mental health providers in your area.

- Do I (or does my family member or friend), have any risk factors for depression?

- Am I (or is my family member or friend) experiencing any symptoms of depression?

- Do I (or does my family member or friend) have co-occurring disorders?

  ○ Have I (or has my family member or friend) been utilizing substances to feel better and manage my symptoms of mental illness?

  ○ Has my (or my family members or friends) substance use let to symptoms of mental illness?

  ○ Do I (or does my family member or friend) need integrated mental health and substance abuse treatment?

- Am I (or is my family member or friend) fearful and scared to see a doctor about what I am experiencing due to fear and stigma?

- Am I (or is my family member or friend):

- at risk for suicide?

- having any warning signs for suicide?

- having any thoughts of suicide?

Chapter 2

Recovery: Drafting Your Team: Captain, Coach and Teammates

Captain: "a person who is at the head of or in authority over others; chief; leader."

- Dictionary.com (n.d.)

Coach: "a person who teaches and trains the members of a sports team and makes decisions about how the team plays during games."

Teammates: "a fellow member of a team."

-Merriam-Webster Dictionary (2015)

A perspective from Cliff:

My rock bottom with clinical depression began in 1994 and continued until 1997. I had a second career in pro sports, I played the Celebrity Pro Golf Tour for 15 years and I was a founder of the Celebrity Players Tour (CPT). In all, I played over 100 events for prize money. My career included two wins and a scoring average of 74.9 strokes around. What it all adds up to is that it was pretty generous to me as I won over $300,000 on the tour.

Once again, skill continued to be very important to me and gave me the choice for success. Early into my golf career, my skills started to leave me. I had my own way of playing that was very unorthodox. When my game began to slump, I felt lost. I was reliving the trauma of losing my tennis game. Let me say again that for me, skill is what I have based my entire professional life around. Feeling this loss for a second time put me under, I was losing hope. After struggling with my golf game and devastating symptoms for three years, I became non-functional in the fall of 1996. For months I couldn't sleep but an hour or two a night. I played golf only a couple days a week, down from seven days a week and had to force myself to play those couple days because I wanted to keep some of my skills if I could but I had lost hope. I stayed home all day. I put black trash bags over my windows so I did not know what time of day it was. I didn't drive my car. I was too tired and didn't feel capable. I cried a lot of the day.

Even with really bad depression it is possible to still lead what looks like a pretty normal life. Your job, family occasions and social functions are all done with your "mask" on. You can "hide" your depression pretty well and I did that from 1994 until the fall of 1996. I played CPT golf events and even had some very good results - I was entered to play the Dan Marino Celeb Classic at Weston Hills in Fort Lauderdale, Florida in January of 1996 that had $200,000 in prize money attached to it. I was so sick and didn't know how I was going to get on the plane to Florida. Somehow I did and the five days in Fort Lauderdale were surreal. I went to the events and parties and played the event. When I was not "on," my off hours were spent in my hotel room crying most of the time with the drapes shut tightly. My wife at the time read me Bible verses as I held her hand. Clinical depression had me firmly in the grasps yet the oddest thing was I finished seventh out of 75 other celebrities in the event with scores of 74, 74 and 74 – that is good golf! Good golf or not, I was very sick. The rest of that year I played four other tournaments and I had very good results even though I was so ill.

The depression was constant, never letting up. I was reaching pain levels I didn't know existed. I was on the downward spiral and did not know how to stop it. My tournament results were pretty good but I felt my skills were evaporating and I was trying hard but feeling worse every day. Hope was in the past, out of my reach.

December of 1996 was my rock bottom. My family was to celebrate Christmas as we always did on Christmas Eve. As my parents and sister came through the front door of our house I broke into tears and went to my darkened bedroom and shut the door. I simply could not go on, I had lost my fight. For the three years up to that point I fought hard to keep going. I used all my competitive skills to overcome what had become my toughest match ever but that time I was stopped in my tracks. My dad always taught me to change my losing game but I didn't know how to do that with this game. He also taught me to "never, ever give up" but I was hanging by a thread, I was ready to give up.

On January 2, 1997 I saw my dermatologist to have an area of skin

cancer removed. Although I was not sure what would happen when I walked into my appointment that day, it would be the beginning of my recovery. My team was starting to take shape and treatment for my disease was in sight.

Before you select and draft the top-rated players for your recovery team, understanding recovery, its purpose and process, is fundamental. The concept of recovery from mental illness has not always been an element of treatment historically, yet there is a firm foundation and roots in writing and research from the mid-1980's addressing recovery and its importance to obtain optimal mental health. The concept and term "recovery" decisively became part of a greater, wide spread conversation in the 1990's when William Anthony defined recovery. Anthony stated that recovery is "a deeply personal, unique process of changing one's attitudes, values, feelings, goals, skills and/ or roles. It is a way of living a satisfying, hopeful, and contributing life even with limitations caused by the illness. Recovery involves the development of new meaning and purpose in one's life as one grows beyond the catastrophic effects of mental illness." Since then, numerous definitions have emerged and recovery has taken a firm hold as an essential, central element of treatment for mental health issues.

The concept of recovery is a familiar one in the world of substance abuse treatment and has strong roots in helping individuals' battle the challenges of substance use and abuse issues. The mental health arena has researched the effectiveness of recovery and adopted some basic tenants, yet developed new areas that align more directly with an individual living with a mental illness.

Experts in the mental health and recovery fields have identified principles that are fundamental in the success of one's recovery process. The American Psychological Association (APA) has endorsed the identified 10 core principles that underpin a recovery orientation. These were agreed on at a 2004 National Consensus Conference on Mental Health Recovery and Mental Health Systems Transformation convened by SAMHSA, patients, health-care professionals, researchers and others. These core principles include *self-direction, individualized and person-centered, empowerment, holistic, nonlinear, strengths based, peer support, respect, responsibility and hope.* Let me explain each of these core principles a bit further for a comprehensive understanding of their importance.

Self-direction focuses on the path to recovery being determined by the consumer.

Individualized and person-centered emphasizes that recovery has many pathways emerging from individuals' strengths as well as needs, choices, experiences and culture.

Empowerment provides choice, choice in making decision and choosing options as well as full participation by consumers in all that impacts them.

Individuals' recovery must be *holistic* and to center on one's whole being including mind, body, spirit and community.

Recovery is *nonlinear*; it is a process of continual growth of which setbacks and learned experience enhance the one's growth.

Strengths-based recovery focuses and builds a foundation on one's strengths.

Peer support from others is instrumental in one's recovery journey.

Respect is a critical part of consumers' recovery with acceptance and appreciation given by society, one's community and providers and systems of care.

One's own self-care and recovery journey are the *responsibility* of the consumer.

Hope is essential, "recovery's central, motivating message is a better future - that people can and do overcome obstacles," according to the APA.

Hope. The last core principle listed is hope yet arguably is the No. 1 core principle of focus. Everyone needs hope in their lives and when someone is facing a mental illness, hope itself is essential. Hope is also necessary to be able to incorporate the nine other core recovery principles into one's life – without hope, one struggles to see purpose and meaning in life. What is so essential about recovery is the crucial aspect that if an individual has hope, support, and education one can see beyond the bullying and lies of the illness and live a life full of meaning, purpose and value while managing symptoms of depression.

Recovery is a deeply personal journey that one must navigate and practice with a team and we know that every successful team has a captain, coach, players and teammates. As you choose and draft your team, you _MUST_ have a team captain, obtain a skilled coaching staff and have players and teammates that bring diverse skills and talents to the game and rally around you to ensure and support your growth and success beyond your illness. The captain of your team is _YOU_...you need to be responsible for the strategy and the mobilization of your teammates as you play the "game" of recovery. Although we know games and seasons end, the recovery process is ongoing and changes based on your needs. So as the captain, you must have your team in place in order to take on the opponents that come your way on your recovery journey. Your coaching staff will include your doctors, social workers, mental health providers, pharmacists, and community resources. These coaches will train and direct you in the best way possible to manage your symptoms and assist you in your recovery process. They have the expertise and tools necessary to provide you the information you need to be an effective captain and strategize and mobilize your teammates. Your players and teammates include the people in your life who support, honor and love you in some way and are recruited based on different needs you have including one's partner, spouse, family member(s), friends, ministers, pastors and rabbi's, employers, work peers, workout buddies, etc. Your team will change over the years as you analyze the strategy and strength of your changing opponent (depression) requiring you to manage who you will need to reach out to and bring in as new recruits.

"In my tennis career I had great coaches and others who helped me in areas I needed help with. I felt more confident and performed better when I got help. I played 1,500 pro matches in 500 events all over the word. I wanted to know all about each opponent I played. I had a game plan every time, I wanted to win... Wanna win? Get good advice!"

- *Cliff Richey, 2014,*
San Angelo Standard Times

Successful progress in your recovery journey requires having the 10 core recovery principles as a permanent part of your playbook and integrated into your strategy. Your coaches, players and teammates, as well as your fans, all need to know and understand these core principles to effectively support you in your recovery journey.

Chapter 2 "Scorecard"
(Ways to know more)

Below are some topics to consider asking yourself (or your family member or friend) to assist you in drafting your team and getting support as you (or your family member or friend) work to conquer your opponent, depression.

- What does my (or my family members or friends) team look like?

  - Who is my (or my family member s or friends) coach?

  - Who are my (or my family members or friends) teammates?

  - What is my (or my family members or friends) team strategy?

- What does recovery mean to me (or my family member or friend)?

- How do the 10 core principles of recovery help me (or my family member or friend) along my journey?

- What is my (or my family members or friends) recovery plan?

- Have you (or your family member or friend) lost hope in your battle of depression?

Chapter 3

Treatment: The Ball Is In Your Court

The ball is in your court: "…to indicate who has the responsibility or opportunity for further action."

- Merriam-Webster Dictionary (2015)

A perspective from Cliff:

"Change a losing game." My coach, my dad, taught me that. In tennis, the score tells you if you are losing and I've been down, way down, in many matches and came back to win. I was sort of the "comeback kid" on tour. The hard part to changing a losing game is you have to be fully engaged in the match; if you are losing it's easy to lose "heart" and to go quietly. That's where my dad's advice of "never, ever, ever give up" became my mantra. A winner's mind set has to always be focused on a way to come back and win no matter how tough the situation – that mindset allows for recovery and giving up ensures defeat.

Walking into my skin doctor's office in January of 1997 was the start of my comeback treatment for clinical depression. There is hope. There is recovery. Here I was, Cliff Richey, a three-time world champion – two Davis Cups and one ITF Grand Prix points championship win – with enough money in the bank, a home that was paid for and a great family...and I was non-functional! That day I poured my heart out to my dermatologist who was also a good family friend. I told him I felt "bummed out" and I wasn't playing golf much anymore. My sleep was erratic and I had low energy. I didn't want to be around other people; I was short tempered and constantly feeling sad. I learned that day that during his medical training, my doctor spent one year learning on the behavioral health unit as part of his residency and so he knew what my symptoms meant. He let me talk and later he told my wife "Cliff has clinical depression and needs to be on antidepressant medication." My wife told me what he had said to her and I jumped off the chair and called his house. "Call in the prescription"

I told my friend and what he said next can change people's lives..." Cliff if you are willing to admit that you have clinical depression and want treatment, you are half way there." There is hope. There is recovery. You have to accept the fact of clinical depression and then want treatment.

I was glad for the diagnosis and I know I had my opponent identified. Somehow our society allows you to be sick from the Adam's apple down but Adam's apple up – uh oh – you should be able to control that yourself. That part of you can't be medically ill!!! Really? Same DNA, same cells as the rest of your body. It's still you. That part can get sick. Denial of Arthur Ashe hitting 30 aces against me doesn't change the fact that he can do that. My job is to not give up and to change a losing game but to accept he is serving those aces and adopt a new game plan. Like I said, I have lived knowing how to win tennis matches and I have also lived in winning against depression.

I call recovery and treatment "my three-legged stool of recovery." The legs are...

1) antidepressant medication - I take my medications every day

2) cognitive therapy – thinking right to beat my opponent

3) a healthy lifestyle - As part of my training to win I slept, ate and worked out properly.

These three key components are the baseline for winning and wellness.

Let me give you more detail on my three-legged stool. Antidepressants are not a "cover the problem pill." They are not a last resort and you don't get "prone" to them and need more of the drug as you go forward. They are not like valium, alcohol, marijuana or cocaine that are "cover-the-problem" drugs that are *depressants* and create depression. Researchers don't know all they would like to know about clinical depression but what they do know is that antidepressants correct a chemical imbalance in the brain that is part of the disease. I say all of this because a lot of people don't know what drugs for depression actually do. These drugs can be compared to insulin for diabetes.

I will now tell you my story and experience with my anti-depressant medication. Besides my dermatologist, I sought treatment from my internist and psychologist. I first tried what was considered a therapeutic dose of medication - 50 mg of Zoloft. After three days, I was nauseous and felt wired and realized I couldn't take that much medication. My teammates, which included my pharmacist (who can have great advice!) cut my dose to 15 mg and we slowly increased the dose over a three-month period. Everyone is different and a lot of people can start feeling improvement of mood in a couple of weeks; not me, but I stuck with it. I wasn't feeling any better as the weeks wore on and increased the dose about every 10 days when I was finally able to tolerate 75 mg after several months of hanging in there. I started to feel some serenity come over me and it was like a dark cloud starting to break up and some sun was creeping through. It had seemed like forever but I knew the medicine was starting to work.

Over the weeks and months that followed, my team consulted with me and we eventually settled on a daily dose of 200 mg. In the beginning I had several side effects including dry mouth and lips, bloating and constipation and some loss of libido. Those side effects for the most part abated as my body needed an adjustment period. Compared to the therapeutic help the meds give me, the side effects are for me a minor inconvenience. I have been on this medication for 18 years and for me, it has been the key to my recovery. To recap my experience, it takes time for medication to work, it is not immediate. One might have to try several different drugs to find the one for you. That may be frustrating but that is the way it is. I was so thankful and found strategies to use against this stubborn opponent. Correct dosage is vital and your team will help you with that. It is important to take your medication consistently at prescribed times and to not miss doses. How long you take the medication varies based on individuals. My team and I have decided that I will stay on the medication for life. The best research informs that this was the best protocol for me.

The second leg of my recovery stool is cognitive therapy. What? Yeah, if you are like me you are saying "What the heck is that??" Cognitive therapy in simple language is locker room lingo for a pep talk, game plan and the correct mental process to win. It's also studying and understanding your foe to know all you can about them before going onto the court. Whether it was John McEnroe or clinical depression, I wanted to know everything I could about them so as to formulate my game plan, a playbook. The player has to be very proactive in studying and learning to formulate the playbook. You are the captain. A good psychologist is a coach but _YOU_ have to be proactive and use all available resources to study as well.

The third leg of my stool is lifestyle. Research shows a healthy body is good for a healthy mind and experts agree that sleep is vital to good mind and body health. Nutrition is also important (yes, mom was right!) as well as exercise as

a part of your program. Your team can help you know what exercise is good for you. My exercise routine was to hit golf balls for two or three hours about 3-4 days a week – hitting my own balls and then walking to pick them up – all great exercise that I did in addition to walking 2-4 miles, several days a week. This is my experience and my lifestyle.

I am winning the battle against clinical depression and I have confidence of victory over this bully and liar.

As you navigate your treatment process and recovery path, it is essential that you are aware of and know what your options for treatment include. Every person's treatment and recovery path is unique to them and for their needs yet there are some standards of care with treatment options as practice and research indicate. Treatment strategies that emerge include the areas of pharmacotherapy (medication), psychotherapy (accessing support through counseling) and lifestyle choices (sleep, eat, drink, exercise, etc.). These are essential strategies for effective treatment and a successful path of recovery. The National Alliance on Mental Illness (NAMI) supports these strategies suggesting that "with early detection, diagnosis and a treatment plan consisting of medication, psychotherapy and lifestyle choices, many people get better. But left untreated, depression can be devastating, both for the people who have it and for their families."

After finally learning what is going on and being provided with a name for what you are experiencing, a diagnosis for your symptoms, treatment can begin. Beginning treatment can feel overwhelming, complicated and uncomfortable, you will most likely feel like an amateur and will need to work diligently in your efforts to overcome the illness and become a champion. There is no ace that will make you a champion but there are effective and successful treatment strategies that work along with your talented and skilled team. Navigating and determining _YOUR_ individual and basic strategies for integration into your treatment regimen is imperative for you and your team moving forward to dominate this fierce opponent.

In the treatment process, you may be referred to as a client, peer, consumer or a patient. Currently the standard term of choice seems to be consumer or peer so to ensure consistency the term consumer will be utilized as we move forward. Treatment requires a detailed playbook of strategy and moves including pharmacotherapy, psychotherapy and recovery that is evidence based and individually applied to ensure efficacy.

Strategy 1: Pharmacotherapy (medication)

In treating and managing depression, pharmacotherapy, and the use of medications as a form of treatment/therapy (also called drug therapy at times) is the first strategy to consider and develop to begin managing your symptoms as quickly as possible. Essentially, medications to treatment mental illness can be compared to insulin for treating diabetes as an example. Both treatments are necessary for the body to be healthy – one addressing blood sugar imbalance and the other treating a chemical imbalance in one's brain. Understanding that there are medications specifically made for addressing depressive symptoms is helpful. Each person experiencing depression is unique making it necessary for individualized pharmacotherapy treatments regarding type and dosage of medication to effectively reduce symptoms and provide ongoing treatment management. There are many terms that you will read and hear when you begin to research medication treatment options. Although all are important for you to understand as you speak to your medical provider, here are several more common terms including therapeutic dosage, efficacy, titration and drug metabolism, defined for you as you begin your education on medications.

According to the Farlex Partner Medical Dictionary, a *therapeutic dosage* refers to the "amount of medication required to produce the desired outcome." *Efficacy* is related to impact on symptom reduction and ongoing management. Mosby's Medical Dictionary defines *titration* as an "incremental increase in drug dosage to a level that provides the optimal therapeutic effect." The National Institute of Health defines *drug metabolism* as "the chemical alteration of a medicine by the body."

It is essential to gain as much information as possible about medications for treatment so one can understand the many classifications and how they work with regard to drug metabolizing, medication combinations, effectiveness and maintenance. Medications that are prescribed to treat symptoms of depression are called anti-depressants. Anti-depressant medications have several classifications allowing for a better effectiveness due to the targeted focus of the medication. The United States Food and Drug Administration (USFDA) outlines the classifications of anti-depressants as follows: Monoamine oxidase inhibitors (MAOIs), Selective serotonin reuptake inhibitors (SSRIs), Serotonin and norepinephrine reuptake inhibitors (SNRIs), and Tricyclics – tetracyclic antidepressants - (TSAs).

The primary function of antidepressants is to balance out moods, reduce symptoms of depression and improve functioning by focusing on brain chemicals called neurotransmitters. Specific focus is on serotonin, norepinephrine and dopamine to balance and regulate the chemical imbalance that exists within individuals who experience depression.

Each different classification of medication influences different neurotransmitters in particular ways. SSRIs focus on increasing the production of serotonin in the brain. MAOIs provide a blockage of monoamine oxidase, an enzyme that breaks down neurotransmitters allowing the neurotransmitter to remain active in the brain. Research on antidepressant medications is ongoing, allowing for a more comprehensive understanding of the precise mechanism of action on an individual's brain. This research allows for new and improved medications with lower side effect potential and greater efficacy.

Monoamine oxidase inhibitors (MAOIs) represent the oldest class of antidepressant medications. These medications have heightened efficacy with individuals experiencing "atypical" depression. Atypical depression refers to an individual experiencing the opposite symptoms of the typical symptoms of depression, such as having an increased appetite and sleep needs rather than decreased appetite and sleep. MAOI's can assist with decreasing feelings of anxiousness and/or panic as well as other specific symptoms. Nardil (phenelzine) and Parnate (tranylcypromine) are several examples of MAOIs.

Some of the newest and most popular antidepressants are called reuptake inhibitors. What does reuptake mean? "It's the process in which neurotransmitters are naturally absorbed back into nerve cells in the brain," according to WebMD.com in the article *How Antidepressants Work*. "A reuptake inhibitor prevents this from happening. Instead of getting reabsorbed, the neurotransmitter stays -- at least temporarily -- in the gap between the nerves, called the synapse."

There are several types of reuptake inhibitors. There are *selective serotonin reuptake inhibitors (SSRIs)* which target serotonin and medications such as Fluoxetine (Prozac), Sertraline (Zoloft), Escitalopram (Lexapro), Paroxetine (Paxil), and Citalopram (Celexa) are some of the most commonly prescribed SSRIs for depression. Most are available in generic versions at lower costs. There is also serotonin *and norepinephrine reuptake inhibitors (SNRIs)* and they block the reuptake of both serotonin and norepinephrine assisting with the reduction of depressive symptoms. Venlafaxine (Effexor) and Duloxetine (Cymbalta) are examples of SNRIs. Wellbutrin (Bupropion) is called a *norepinephrine and dopamine reuptake inhibitors (NDRIs)* and is not considered a class as there is only one drug that does this.

Tricyclics are older antidepressants called tetracyclic antidepressants (TCAs). These medications are powerful and have serious potential side effects so are prescribed much less frequently today. Elavil (Amitriptyline), Tofranil (Imipramine) and Nortriptyline (Pamelor) are several examples of TCAs.

The side effects of some medications for depression often pose difficulties for individuals and their desire to take them or their ongoing compliance. Specifically, some MAOI's, which may cause dietary problems and TSAs may cause one to experience dry mouth and constipation. Due to these side effects, doctors often prescribe the newer, second generation of antidepressants (SSRIs) as the side effects are often less of a problem. Further, these medications have a lower overdose risk with this classification than other antidepressants. It is important to note that even with the newer second generation antidepressants one can have side effects including issues such as weight gain and reduce libido.

Individuals deciding to take antidepressants should specifically address the issue of side effects with their physician. More times than not, the benefits of the medications far outweigh the challenges of the side effects as one works to move forward in their recovery and live a healthy lifestyle.

As you determine the medications that are best for you, the relationship you have with your doctor is imperative. It is suggested to have an ongoing dialogue as long as you are on medications, which may be for a defined or unknown period of time. Asking specific questions initially, and as you continue on medication, is critical. What questions should you ask? Helpful questions might include:

- How will the medication(s) treat my symptoms?

- What are the differences between the medications – what should each medication specifically do?

- What is the dosage of the medication(s)?

- How often should the medication(s) be taken?

- How long will I have to take the medication(s)?

- How long does the medication take to begin working?

- What are the side effects of the medication(s)?

- Are there any dietary restrictions due to the medicatlon(s)?

- How will the medication interact with other medication(s) I am taking?

"I've had some depressive dips, but not once have I said, 'Uh-oh, the Zoloft's not working anymore' You're getting into real dangerous territory there. This is, potentially, a real can of worms. Then all of a sudden you're wanting to switch medications. It's the drive-thru or 'quick fix' mentality. Your antidepressant can

only do so much for you! It would be like a diabetic eating a double cheese burger and a malt and then when they feel bad, thinking their insulin isn't working. 'The problem might not be your medicine, dude. Look in the mirror and see what if it might be you!' Some day they will invent a drug that can keep you from crashing. I believe that. I would see no reason at all, with the miraculous things that have happened in medicine why that would not be possible. But it's going to be much easier to come up with a pill that keeps you from falling than one that allows you to crash normally. What most depressed people don't realize is that ultimately, you're still going to want a range of emotion. You don't want a pill that keeps you from crashing altogether. You just want one that provides you a parachute."

- Cliff Richey, Acing Depression

Strategy 2: Psychotherapy (counseling)

Psychotherapy is another strategy for your treatment playbook that is essential to partner with pharmacotherapy as a way to reduce symptoms and provide tools to manage thought patterns and behaviors negatively impacting your overall optimal mental health. Many people harbor some stereotypical beliefs regarding psychotherapy leading to misinformation and misunderstanding regarding the reality of this type of treatment and the numerous benefits that it can provide. Psychotherapy might sound scary or intrusive to some and it certainly has its own societal stigma as if someone is going to "psychoanalyze you" or "control you in some way." Dispelling those misconceptions is essential for a greater perspective on how this will fit into your playbook. Therapy and counseling are terms that emerge with regard to this treatment offering and as a generalization are both focused on providing professional assistance to individuals to assist them in the management and resolution of emotional issues. Psychotherapy allows individuals a safe environment to express their concerns, conflicts, and emotions as they work to understand and resolve these issues for improved mental health resulting in increased optimal daily functioning. Psychotherapy goes beyond supportive counseling; it utilizes specific types of what are referred to as evidence based therapies that treat psychological symptoms. Evidence-based therapies are therapeutic techniques that have been proven effective through research.

One of the most well-known, effective and commonly utilized evidence based practices for addressing mental health symptoms includes cognitive behavioral therapy. Cognitive behavioral therapy (CBT) is one of the most effective therapeutic treatments. According to R.C. Wyatt and E.L. Seid in *The Instructor's Manual for Cognitive Behavioral Therapy* CBT "comprises a variety of procedures, such as cognitive restructuring, stress inoculation training, problem solving, skills training, relaxation training and others." Those who have tried classic "talk" therapy find CBT different. CBT is a short-term, collaborative, goal-directed therapy. It's a process that helps the consumer become his or her own therapist. It's structured, makes the best use of the consumer's time, and cost-effective.

CBT starts with education about the consumer's presenting problem, whether that's depression, anxiety, trauma, or substance abuse. For example, if a consumer presents as depressed, the CBT therapist explains how depressed people distort their thinking and think negatively about themselves, the future and the world in general, including other people. Dr. Aaron Beck, who developed CBT, refers to this as "the cognitive triad." The therapist educates the consumer on how the consumer's ineffective coping skills reinforce those negative thoughts, with a goal of normalizing and depersonalizing the illness.

Initial CBT sessions allow the therapist to lay a framework for the future by teaching the cognitive model. Though it sounds intimidating, the concept is simple: a person's thoughts and behaviors influence their mood, not a particular event. For example, if my friend doesn't immediately return a phone call, I may think, "He's mad at me; we must not be friends anymore." But actually, he may be in class or a meeting, asleep, or otherwise unavailable. My reaction to the event changes my mood, not the event itself.

A CBT therapist also works with the consumer to identify concrete therapy goals. These goals act as a roadmap, in part so both parties know when therapy should end. The therapist and consumer set goals by asking, "If I weren't so depressed and anxious, what would I be doing? What would life look like?" Five short-term and five long-term goals are usually a good start. The goal list is not static; it is a living document. As therapy progresses, some goals are reached, others become unimportant, and new ones can be added.

Though CBT includes a thorough assessment of the consumer's history and presenting problem, the therapist starts with the here-and-now and works backwards. The therapist tries to gain an understanding of the consumer's belief system, looking for clues to identify the consumer's core beliefs and how those beliefs were established. That can lead to immediate relief by identifying the consumer's automatic thoughts. These thoughts typically are fleeting and not subject to logical analysis, and often pop into the mind so rapidly we're not even aware of what we tell ourselves. If I'm depressed, these automatic thoughts tend to be overly negative, causing me to "beat myself up." So early on, CBT teaches the importance of paying close attention to mood. When my mood shifts and I feel anxiety grow, or I become more depressed, CBT teaches me to ask myself, "What was I just thinking? What was going through my mind when I felt that emotion?" Once we identify what we tell ourselves, we can evaluate the accuracy of these thoughts.

CBT is not just about positive thinking; it's about *accurate* thinking. It identifies "thinking errors," or patterns of thought that contribute to issues such as depression. Thinking errors involve assumptions we make, and how we fill in a lack of facts with negative information. Some of the most common responses to thinking errors are reliance on mind reading or fortune telling, or a tendency to "catastrophize" or overgeneralize. Tunnel vision also is a thinking error. Tunnel vision is seeing only the subset of information that confirms the negative point of view, and filters out or ignores contrary data. Other thinking errors include magnification and minimization, which involve making accurate information more or less important in the mind than in reality. The last set of thinking errors are absolutes They include rigid views of oneself, others, or life in general that are overly harsh, perfectionistic, or uncompromising. This includes categorical thinking, a belief that everything is good or bad, success or failure. It also includes labeling, or global critical labels for self or others (stupid, lazy, etc.), as well as "shoulds" and "musts," which are rigid rules about how people should act or things should be. In CBT, the therapist and consumer work to identify, evaluate, and avoid these thinking errors.

How does CBT combat these automatic thoughts? One way is to look for evidence for and against those thoughts. For example, if an automatic thought is, "I'm a bad father," the therapist will help the consumer look for ways he is and is not a bad father. This can also help combat the negative, distorted thoughts of depressed consumers, and give useful information to add to the goal list, such as, "Spend more time with son and daughter." Evidence may help the consumer realize the negative thought is inaccurate, find ways to change it, or help find ways to gather more information to invalidate a negative thought.

As CBT sessions progress, common themes typically emerge for each consumer. These common themes usually point to schemas, or core beliefs. The best way to make long-term changes to automatic thoughts is to combat negative core beliefs, such as "I'm worthless" or "I'm helpless" or "I'm unlovable." We try to minimize a client's negative core beliefs, while identifying and maximizing the positive ones. Most CBT begins with weekly, one-hour sessions. CBT is not just about an hour in the office. CBT has homework. Homework helps the consumer practice what they have learned and apply it to the "real world." And as the consumer reaches therapy goals, the sessions decrease until therapy is over. The final sessions work on relapse prevention, with later "booster" or "maintenance" sessions if depression or anxiety returns.

In order to gain the most from the therapeutic process, having the "right" "coach" in your treatment provider is imperative for therapy to be an effective piece of the treatment process; finding that "right" fit with a provider can be intimidating and difficult to navigate. As the team captain, you must analyze all your teammates and players and recruit a provider that best fits your expectations and meets your needs.

There are multiple steps required in finding that successful coach you will have as your therapist.

The first step in the process of finding a therapist necessitates creating a list of qualified psychotherapy providers in your area including licensed clinical social workers and licensed clinical professional counselors as well as psychologists. Each of these qualified providers have gained the skills through education and experience to work with depression yet some have more experience and expertise that might meet your needs more optimally and offer a greater lead in your set, match, game! The list you develop could come from an internet search, referrals from friends, family or a community resource if available. You can find a CBT therapist near you through the Academy of Cognitive Therapy website, www.academyofct. org. Once you have identified the providers you believe will be good coaches, you will need to verify their credentials with your state professional license regulation site to ensure they are correctly and currently licensed in your state to provide the treatment you are seeking. After verifying the credentials, it is necessary to confirm the provider(s) you have chosen is (are) authorized to bill your insurance (whether you have public or private insurance) or is willing to negotiate a fee that you can pay if you are uninsured or they are not set up to take insurance payments. Additionally, you want to make sure the location and hours of availability for service meet your needs on an ongoing basis.

Having established foundational aspects of credentials, payment and availability, the next step is ensuring that you have the "best fit" with your therapist and they have the skills and approach that meets your needs. To accomplish getting this best "fit," a "try-out" must take place by interviewing your potential provider.

Sharing your expectations will assist in creating the best connection and therapeutic relationship you can have with them. Both parties should expect certain elements for the best assurance of a successful therapeutic relationship. The elements that both parties should bring to the table in the therapeutic relationship include respect, honesty, understanding and commitment. Additionally, it is imperative your therapist brings empathy along with effective and appropriate skills to meet your needs including effective listening and communication, appropriate boundary development, confidentiality, ethical behavior, patience, problem-solving, and critical thinking. As the consumer, you should be prepared to communicate openly to share your needs, explore your strengths and weaknesses and address your problems.

Throughout the therapeutic process it is important for you to engage to the best of your ability by being prepared for each session, providing feedback on your progress all to gain the most out of each session. Input into your goals and the length of your treatment is a must as you are the captain of your team and know yourself best.

"Don't forget the role of cognitive therapy. Don't rely on antidepressant medication alone."

- Cliff Richey, Acing Depression

Strategy 3: Recovery (healing)

Recovery begins the moment you commit to accepting your illness as a part of who you are and engage in treatment to become healthy and have optimal functioning. Recovery is a life-long process that allows for twists and turns and changes as your wants and needs vary based on your life circumstances. Recovery does not just happen, it is a process that requires time, patience, commitment and _WORK_ and takes your entire team to be successful. Recovery must always remain your focus and in the forefront as the goal of your treatment.

During your recovery process, the creation of a Wellness Recovery Action Plan (WRAP) will prove invaluable help as you take control of your illness and create our team strategy to win games, matches and Grand Slams. WRAP is a tool created by mental health advocate and mental illness survivor Mary Ellen Copeland that identifies a plan for you to know yourself and allow others to know your actions, behaviors and wishes you when you are ill and when you are well.

According to Copeland, WRAP is "a self-designed prevention and wellness process that anyone can use to get well, stay well and make their life the way they want it to be. It was developed in 1997 by a group of people who were searching for ways to overcome their own mental health issues and move on to fulfilling their life dreams and goals. It is now used extensively by people in all kinds of circumstances, and by health care and mental health systems all over the world to address all kinds of physical, mental health and life issues...WRAP will help you discover your own simple, safe Wellness Tools, develop a list of things to do every day to stay as well as possible, identify upsetting events, early warning signs and signs that things have gotten much worse and, using Wellness Tools, develop action plans for responding at these times, guide you through the process of developing a Crisis Plan or Advance Directive, and introduce you to Post Crisis Planning."

WRAP focuses on having a Wellness Toolbox and the development of the areas of a *daily maintenance plan*, identification of your *triggers* and *early warning signs*, gaining an understanding of *when things are breaking down*, developing a *crisis plan* and a *post crisis plan*. The development of all of these areas will come together to create your WRAP plan that you will utilize, change, and enhance to support you in your recovery journey. Here are some great quotes that you may find helpful in understanding aspects of WRAP and how they relate to your recovery:

> *"Lack of patience is a warning sign. I get frustrated quicker. I'm very critical of other people. When I'm going into one of my depressive episodes, I start to scoff... If you can learn to identify warning signs, they're not as threatening." - Cliff Richey, Acing Depression*

"Triggers don't have to be catastrophic. They can be anything. It's just a weakness you have. You have a debit in that column." - Cliff Richey, Acing Depression

"In times of crisis, you also need to focus more on things like diet and exercise. I call it reaching into your bag of tricks. Do things to compensate for your injury."

- Cliff Richey, Acing Depression

Chapter 3 "Scorecard"
(Ways to know more)

Below are some topics to consider asking yourself (or your family member or friend) to assist in your treatment plan for depression.

- Is medication appropriate for me (or my family member or friend)? Where do I (or does my family member or friend) learn about medication options?

- Am I (or is my family member or friend) interested in cognitive therapy? How do I (or does my family member or friend) think that will assist in my treatment?

- What is my (or my family members or friends) current lifestyle?

○ What are my (or my family members or friends) healthy and unhealthy lifestyle habits?

○ What do I (or does my family member or friend) need to change to become healthier?

• Do I (or does my family member or friend) want to create a WRAP Plan?

Chapter 4

Maintenance: Moves In Your Playbook

Moves: "to go from one place or position to another."

Playbook: "a stock of usual tactics or methods."

- Merriam-Webster Dictionary (2015)

A perspective from Cliff:

As you can see by now I feel my competitive skills learning in my pro tennis career have also been used to battle my clinical depression. I believe my skills are needed in both! I found out pretty quickly in my long tennis career that good skills enable me to win at the highest level. But winning early on was just the start of a long career. I had to be constantly vigilant to maintain those hard-won skills. It became a lifestyle of workouts, off court training, proper diet and good rest. I also knew my "competitive thinking skills" would be the biggest key to winning. Having a proper "mental game" was an ongoing process. My coach (who was my dad) was always monitoring my outlook on and off the court. I learned my early success was not going to guarantee future victories, it was a process. Physical and mental maintenance were both key to my long career. To me, longevity is a hallmark of great careers.

Winning against clinical depression is a skill that requires maintenance.

In risking being repetitive, I want to say to you again – you and you alone must decide to seek help. Accept the fact you have a bonafide disease that you decide to overcome. I had a great team around me in pro tennis and I was the one who walked out on the court and competed. You are the one who accepts the fact that clinical depression is your opponent you can win against.

So your winning career against clinical depression has started and now you want longevity. As I have said, I personally have what I call my three legged stool in my recovery that I used early on and now try to maintain. Think of it this way – it is not win one and done!

It's winning a lot and maintaining. You maintain by using those hard won skills in an ongoing methodical effort.

One leg of my stool is my daily dose of my SSRI to keep my serotonin flow in my brain to put me on a level playing field with others. The second leg of using my learned skills of cognitive therapy is kept in my handy toolbox. Thankfulness, humor, moderation, following the golden rule and seeking excellence and not perfection are a part of this leg. A lot of people, as I have said before, are simply uninformed. The very common opinion of many is that antidepressants are nothing more than a last resort to get better, that it is the "cover over" pill or simply a "feel good" pill. Science has proven this is not true. In your brain image, two cells connect by what is called a synapse. That's science talk for a pathway from one cell to the other. In a normal brain serotonin is released by a cell into the pathway or synapse and it flows to the other cell. This smooth flow helps create a normal, healthy system. In a brain with depression the cells releasing the serotonin literally sucks up the serotonin and connection to the other cell is disrupted, hence the name of the class of drug I take –SSRI. On the other hand, let me repeat that alcohol, valium, marijuana, cocaine and heroin are actual depressants. Feel good for a little while but in the long term they make clinical depression worse and can actually create depression. A lot of untreated clinically depressed people self -medicate these "feel good" drugs. Again, these are not my opinions; this comes from the best clinical researchers in the field.

Cognitive therapy can sound very technical and intimidating especially when I was so sick and non-functional, but it is not really. I learned to "think" better in several different ways. I had a year of counseling and I read a lot on what clinical depression was – getting to know my opponent. In simple terms, cognitive theory is learning to live and think better, healthier thoughts and healthier living. We all need to reorganize sometimes. The best clinical research shows that negative, bad thoughts can actually create a sick brain. Healthy, good thoughts can reverse that disease process. Journaling is another form of mental therapy – getting your thoughts down on paper can be very therapeutic.

It is reasonable to say that once the proper medications are doing their job it's easier to get good cognitive theory to sink in. Meds can clear the foggy thinking to absorb and learn better, healthier thinking skills. The best researchers say there are three treatments for the disease of clinical depression:

1) medication only, that's one protocol

2) cognitive therapy alone

3) the best is a medication and cognitive therapy combination

For me, I've decided to stay on medications. My instincts tell me to do this. It's a winning strategy for me. I don't want to change a winning game.

But the "mental coaches" and research says this can be a good protocol. I also work daily on using my "toolkit." All of the tools I have told you about allows you to see and live life in a healthy, positive way.

Again, good treatment is not a "one and done." I have accepted that I have a chronic disease. For me, it will require daily maintenance for the rest of my life. As I said before, I try to eat a sensible diet, I monitor my stressors and I know I need plenty of good sleep and I exercise five days a week.

You are the one who decides to get well and to feel better. Live a productive life. Have hope for a good future. You are the captain of this healthy life. There is hope. There is recovery. There are no magic words. I was a good pro tennis player, a high school drop out with good street sense but I chose to get well. I chose to accept the informed diagnosis of clinical depression. I chose to get treatment. I wanted to get better and be creative and productive again. I have now had 20 years of very good recovery. You can too.

Extra innings are necessary for continued recovery success as well as specific moves from your playbook to ensure maintenance for managing your illness. There is no cure for depression, but we know that depression is manageable and does not have to limit us as long as there is ongoing maintenance. The purpose of maintenance is to continue the efforts you have started and found successful in managing your depression. Many people engage in treatment with pharmacotherapy and psychotherapy and begin their journey of recovery, yet fail to realize the need for continued maintenance allowing for support and continued growth. This happens because there has been growth and you feel better but putting those tools aside leaves you vulnerable again and separated from your team leading to potential relapse of symptoms and decreased quality of life. Your maintenance now is a _MUST_ and it takes work…Remember, this is your new normal. You need to continue to move forward and keep your health as your priority.

Major Depressive Disorder is an illness that is quite possibly long-term and even lifelong requiring maintenance to actively work to avoid recurrence of symptoms. To foster your successful personal plan, it is recommended that individuals incorporate what is called maintenance psychotherapy and pharmacotherapy together for optimal benefit. This type of psychotherapy is designed to focus on the prevention of recurrence and the potential development of a new depressive episode. Additionally, pharmacotherapy maintenance is an essential piece that in research has shown to reduce the recurrence rate of depression significantly if individuals continue to take antidepressants. This phase will also include continuing to have focus on the 10 core principles of recovery (discussed earlier) and a healthy balanced lifestyle.

Establishing your needs and creating your individualized maintenance plan will require you to involve all members of your team. As the captain, you will have to communicate your needs and perspective with your coaching staff and teammates and listen to their feedback. Your personal plan will evolve over time as you continue to be healthy and your needs change.

Chapter 4 "Scorecard"
(Ways to know more)

Below are some topics to consider asking yourself (or your family member or friend) to assist in the maintenance and continued management of your depression.

- What is my (or my family members or friends) maintenance plan?

- How is my (or my family members or friends) maintenance plan utilized in my recovery?

- Does my (or my family members or friends) team understand the need for maintenance?

- How will I (or my family member or friend) use my team for ongoing support?

- If I (or my family member or friend) "fall off" my maintenance plan, what do I (or my family member or friend) need to do to get back on?

Chapter 5

Acing It...... From Amateur To Champion!

Amateur: "a person who is not skillful at a job or other activity."

Champion: "someone who fights or speaks publicly in support of a person, belief, cause, etc."

- Merriam-Webster Dictionary (2015)

A perspective from Cliff:

You have been in a battle to reclaim your life. You have chosen a great team and executed your playbook. Hey champ, let's go out and continue to be a winner!

Champions go forward with confidence and energy in their family life, work, and friendships. Winners want longevity. My recovery these last 20 years has gotten me back in the game of life. My family relationships are back on an even keel and I can have more patience and can actually feel the natural love we all want with the ones who matter the most. Being emotionally sick with depression is not easy for families and now I truly want to give of myself because they have been such support and comfort through the bad times. For many years I had a selfish life. The pro tennis tour is a weird and selfish life by definition. Throw in clinical depression and dysfunction is always present. I wanted to win over depression for my loved ones because I had been a load on them for 30 years. I can be there for all of them now!

I am a Christian and believe in the golden rule – give unto others and you shall also receive. I also know how healing it has been for me to now be there for my family. After winning my match with depression I've been equipped to have more empathy and compassion. Depression has humbled me. Depression put me in a very selfish mode. I had such pain for so long; I was constantly trying to fix myself. Understandable or not, my family needed more from me. Trust me; it was my biggest incentive to get well.

My best friends supported me and loved me during the dark times. I have three kinds of friends. Those who have fought the battle with depression and speak "my language," those who know it is a real disease and cheer me on and those who are not aware of the disease but still show their love. Let me digress a bit. My advice to family and friends is to get educated about clinical depression. It helps to be able to talk about it with those in the grip of darkness. My dad never had depression but he "knew" about it. He read up on it. He could have empathy for me during our many "heart to hearts." My dad would call me almost every day about 10 am. I'd hear the phone ring and knew it was probably my dad. "How do you feel Clifford?" Love and comfort is truly the best medicine at times. Put your arm around your loved one and simply say "We'll get through this, I love you." I can now do that with family and friends and show them support. It's medicine for the soul.

Recovery and winning over depression has not been a straight line for me, but the trend is an upward path. That is reality. Over these last 20 years I have had dips. I have had days and even weeks of some depression. Even my best year on the pro tennis tour my record had a few losses. Having more wins and a few losses is the reality of a champion, it is recovery! Not recovered! It's winning! Not won and done!

Champions choose to be, it's not bestowed. God gives us the power of choice and I made a choice to try to be a tennis champion. It was at 12 years old and I remember the day I made that choice. The depression sufferer must choose wellness. Nobody can do it for you. That choice is being "all in!" and "100 percent!" (told you I tended to be a perfectionist!) To me, I compare it to concentration; I wasn't on court with a few random thoughts.

Let me tell you a true story. A young high school golfer was a friend of mine. He called me one day and said "Cliff, I need some advice. In my school tournaments I play the first 14 holes real good and then I lose concentration. I'm shooting 77 or 78 instead of close to par. What do I do to concentrate better?" I said, "J.C., picture this scene. You and your girlfriend are out on a beautiful west Texas ranch deer hunting. Your girlfriend accidently shoots herself in the foot and you immediately go into survival mode. You use your belt to help stop the bleeding. You drive in to town with your horn blaring and lights on as fast as you can to the nearest emergency room. Total concentration in every move. You see a bar on the street corner three blocks from the hospital and decide to stop and have a few beers while your girlfriend waits in the car. No way right?! You will absolutely stay focused until you get to the emergency room! Why? Because this is how important it is to you. You will concentrate with tunnel vision until your girlfriend is helped." Concentration on any task is simply related to the simple question "How badly do you want it?" Choose wellness, it's up to you.

Recovery has improved my creative professional life as well. After my three-year breakdown, I got back off the floor and played 12 more years of pro golf and I felt good 80 percent of the time. The other 20 percent I had some depression but those dips have been less potent and less in duration. Continuing my golf allowed me to work my craft and pad my back account a little more! More importantly was the renewed feeling of self-worth and confidence we all need. My tank of hope was being refilled.

Being able to be an advocate for mental health is truly a blessing. I want to help those suffering from clinical depression. I will continue to speak at venues across the country, to break stigmas, educate and to comfort those who suffer.

Clinical depression is a disease and is known to be the most treatable disease of all mental disorders. There is evidence based treatment. Let us all go forward choosing to win and defeat this disease. Never, ever, ever give up.

There _IS_ life beyond depression - a meaningful, fun and interesting life if you choose to live it. It is important to understand that as with other areas of your life, you must give yourself permission and allow room for success and failure without judgment or blame and commit to living the life you want and being the champion you are as you live with depression. Remember, you live with depression, it is _NOT_ your identity, it is _NOT_ who you are.

You began this journey as an amateur with a diagnosis of Major Depressive Disorder feeling scared, confused, hopeless, labeled, stigmatized and empty. Along the way you improved your skills, revealed your talents and gained knowledge. Hope, confidence and power came as you challenged your illness, created your team and worked to win your Grand Slam against depression. You became the champion. On this journey you realized that depression is a bully and a liar yet you found you had options to hear the truth. You became involved and gained strength to challenge the bully and dispel those lies by taking power and control back. Continue to know your strengths, weaknesses and limitations, then trust your own judgment – you are the captain of your team and you know _YOU_ best.

You may be someone who experiences an episode of clinical (major) depression or you may have recurring episodes of depression. Adapting to the new normal of life with depression is essential. Part of that adaptation is learning and accepting that this new normal offers challenges and potential barriers yet limitless opportunities also exist. _YOU_ create _YOUR_ new normal and defeat your opponent game, set, match...you win!

Continuing to perfect your "game" will be essential. As you play games and matches in your recovery journey, you will "fault" and "volley" and "lob." You will even have the "advantage" and win some matches at times along the way but your match never ends. A champion must always rally and work to defeat the opponent.

In the appendix of this book are some resources that should prove helpful in your recovery journey. There are two worksheets focusing on suicide – _Reasons to Live_ (appendix A) and _Reasons to Have Hope_ (appendix B). Lastly, _Mental Health and Recovery Resources_ (appendix

C) is a list and description resources and websites where you can find more information about medications, CBT, support, WRAP, education and advocacy. These resources are a part of your toolkit as you navigate _YOUR_ recovery.

You have made it! You made it through this book and hopefully found support, guidance, information, resources and _HOPE_ as you (or your family member or friend) begin the recovery journey and move away from the grips of depression. Depression is a bully and a liar and has incredible strength and power when left untreated BUT there is life beyond depression and you can have that life. We wish you well on your recovery journey to a healthy and happy life and leave you with some powerful words from Cliff:

"The bottom line is: depression can be beaten. Far worse than losing is not staying out on the court. Depression will tell you it's not worth it to keep fighting, but you don't have to listen to that voice. Listen to what I'm telling you instead. Even if you forget everything else, remember these words: NEVER, EVER, EVER GIVE UP!"

- Cliff Richey, Acing Depression

Chapter 5 "Scorecard"
(Ways to know more)

Below are some topics to consider and assist you (or your family member or friend) in becoming a champion over your depression and.....*Acing it!*

- Reflect on the journey from amateur to champion.

- Envision life beyond depression.

- Continue to perfect my "ace" and become the champion of my illness and keep winning.

- Stay focused and utilize all support systems.

- "Never, ever, ever give up!"

Afterword

Depression is a bully and a liar.

Depression, as with all mental illness, is a public health issue that has resulted out of lack of education, fear and stigma. Individuals experiencing depression are all around us; impacting individuals of all ages, genders, racial and socioeconomic backgrounds. According to NAMI, "an estimated 16 million American adults, almost 7 percent of the population, had at least one major depressive episode last year alone." There are significantly high costs to individuals, families and communities as a result of depression including emotional, financial and relational costs. If we ourselves are not dealing with depression, I am confident we know someone who is.......a family member, peer, friend, or co-worker. If the prevalence of depression is not concerning enough, suicide and its connection to depression is even more troubling and misunderstood.

Suicide and depression have a correlation that many are largely unaware of and is imperative to understand. The American Psychological Association stated that the "possibility of suicidal behavior exists at all times during major depressive episodes," Further, the American Association of Suicidology (AAS) stated "depression is the psychiatric diagnosis most commonly associated with suicide" and if left untreated, depression can lead to other mental health issues occurring at the same time as well as frequent and increased suicide rates. Further, the AAS indicated the lifetime risk of suicide among individuals whose depression is untreated ranges from about 2 percent to 15 percent with depression present in at least 50 percent of all suicides. Individuals suffering from depression are at a higher risk, 25 times higher, for suicide than those without depression. As stated earlier and important to say again, suicide is the 10th leading cause of death among adults in the U.S. and the third leading cause of death among adolescents.

These facts are staggering and real. Depression is a public health issue that must be addressed. Diagnosis and treatment of clinical depression are the first line of defense to ensuring quality of life and reducing the risk suicide. Individuals can and do recover from clinical depression and thoughts of suicide but seeking help is the first step in gaining control over your illness and creating your playbook.

If there is any indication that you or your loved one is at risk for suicide please contact your local hospital, mental health provider crisis line or the National Suicide Prevention Hotline at 1(800) 273-8255 immediately.

Acknowledgements

I would like to offer my thanks and gratitude to my co-author, Mary Garrison, for her great work and enthusiasm for doing this project. My sister, Nancy Richey, for helping me with this book and all of my mental health activism. A special shout out to my good pal Dusty McCoy for his help and expertise. Dusty does amazing work as head of West Texas Counseling and Guidance Center. A big thank you to my pal Allen Fox , PhD and fellow pro tour player. And, of course, I want to thank Randy Walker and New Chapter Press for being my publisher and being in my corner for many years.

-Cliff Richey

I would like to thank Cliff for his friendship and for asking me to collaborate on this book with him. I am humbled and honored to be able to contribute information and resources to individuals and families facing mental illness that my hope is will positively impact those who utilize the information. Cliff and I share our passion for eliminating stigma, ensuring access to effective treatment and educating about mental health and recovery. I am grateful our paths crossed as keynote speakers at the Montana State NAMI Conference…an instant friendship was born and I am a better person for having Cliff in my life.

I would like to thank my life partner, David Horn, and son, Severino Napolitano, for their love and support during this process. Their faith and encouragement in my ability to write this book was steadfast and kept me prodding on when my confidence waivered. Thank you to my father, Michael Garrison, who took valuable time to read, provide edits and suggestions, and discuss my manuscript with me along this journey. Thanks Dad.

Thank you to Kit and Peter Paulin for allowing me to take over their cabin for a week to begin this journey providing a secluded, tranquil place to remove myself from the demands of daily life and focus on writing this book – this is truly where it all began.

-Mary E. Garrison

Reasons To Live

Make a list of reasons to continue living. When you begin to have dark thoughts about life, look over the list to remind yourself of reasons to hold on another day.

Reasons why I shouldn't leave:

_____

_____

_____

People to live for:

_____

_____

_____

Things I would miss:

_____

_____

_____

Experiences I have not yet had:

_____

_____

_____

Things that matter to me:

_____

_____

_____

Reprinted with permission from Monica Ramirez Basco, Ph.D & Guilford Press

Appendix B

Reasons To Have Hope

Make a list of reasons that you believe there might be hope for the future. Resist the urge to tell yourself that there is no hope so why bother. Here are some questions that might help you think of reasons to have hope.

- Are you doing anything differently now that might suggest there is hope for improvement?

- Are the problems that bring you down likely to be temporary? Will they resolve themselves with time?

- Why do other people believe that there is hope for the future?

- Is it possible that you have not given it all of your effort?

- Have you been through times like this before? Have things usually gotten better with time, effort, or patience?

My Reasons for Hope

_____

_____

_____

Reprinted with permission from Monica Ramirez Basco, Ph.D & Guilford Press

Mental Health and Recovery Resources

https://www.nami.org/ - provides information to learn more about mental health conditions, find support and get involved.

http://www.mentalhealthamerica.net/ - provides resources about living well, finding help, getting involved, mental health information, policy and advocacy.

https://copelandcenter.com/ - provides information and resources on wellness and recovery through WRAP.

http://mindovermood.com/ – provides information about Cognitive Behavioral Therapy (CBT) – principles, resources and worksheets and access to CBT certified therapists.

**https://www.nimh.nih.gov/health/topics/
depression/index.shtml** - provides specific
information about depression – definition, signs
and symptoms and treatment.

**http://www.fda.gov/forconsumers/
consumerupdates/ucm095980.htm** - provides
information from the FDA on antidepressant
medication.

**http://www.dbsalliance.org/site/
PageServer?pagename=home** – provides
information and resources from the Depression
and Bipolar Support Alliance.

http://www.mhresources.org/ - provides
information and resources for services within
the community to individuals recovering from
serious mental illness.

http://www.mentalhealth.gov/- provides
information and resources about mental health
– overall information, signs and symptoms and
access to help.

http://www.adaa.org/living-with-anxiety/ask-and-learn/resources - website for the *Anxiety and Depression Association of America* providing information on facts and resources for healthy living.

http://www.helpguide.org/articles/depression/types-of-antidepressants-and-their-side-effects.htm#resources - provides information on types of anti-depressants and side effects.

References

Addis M.E., & Mahalik J.R. (2003). *Men, masculinity, and the contexts of help seeking.* American Psychologist. 58(1):5–14.

amateur (2015). In *Merriam-Webster.com.* Retrieved July 27, 2015, from http://www. merriam-webster.com/dictionary/amateur

American Psychiatric Association. (2013). *Diagnostic and statistical manual of mental disorders* (5th ed.). Washington, DC: Author.

Anthony, W. A. (1993). Recovery from mental illness: The guiding vision of the mental health service system in the 1990s. *Psychosocial Rehabilitation Journal, 16*(4), 11–23.

APA, 2013 article entitled Major Depressive Disorder and the "Bereavement Exclusion". Retrieved on 7/29/15 from http://www.dsm5. org/Documents/Bereavement%20Exclusion%20 Fact%20Sheet.pdf

Basco, M.R. (2015). The Bipolar Workbook: Tools for Controlling your Mood Swings, 2nd Edition. New York: Guilford Press

Blier, P., Keller, M.B., Pollack, M.H., Thase, M.E., Zajecka, J.M., & Dunner, D.L. (2007). *Preventing recurrent depression: long-term treatment for major depressive disorder.* Journal of Clinical Psychiatry. 68(3):e06 bully (2015). In *Merriam-Webster. com*. Retrieved July 27, 2015, from http://www. merriam-webster.com/dictionary/bully

Campbell, F.R., Pre Conference workshop leader for 2014 (Columbus, Ohio) and 2015 (Ft. Worth, Texas) National Loss team Conferences providing loss team training workshops at both events. www.lossteam.com

captain (n.d.). *Dictionary.com Unabridged.* Retrieved July 30, 2015 from Dictionary.com website http://www.dictionary.com/browse/ captain

Center for Substance Abuse Treatment (US). Addressing the Specific Behavioral Health

Needs of Men. Rockville, MD: Substance Abuse and Mental Health Services Administration (US); 2013. (Treatment Improvement Protocol (TIP) Series, No. 56.) 4, Working With Specific Populations of Men in Behavioral Health Settings. Available from: http://www.ncbi.nlm.nih.gov/books/NBK144297/

champion (2015). In *Merriam-Webster.com*. Retrieved July 27, 2015, from http://www.merriam-webster.com/dictionary/champion

coach (2015). In *Merriam-Webster.com*. Retrieved July 27, 2015, from http://www.merriam-webster.com/dictionary/coach

Comer, R. J. (2015). *Abnormal psychology (9th ed.)*. New York: Worth.

Co-occurring Disorders. (2016, March 8). Retrieved June 07, 2016, from http://www.samhsa.gov/disorders/co-occurring

Copeland, M. E., PhD. (2015). WRAP is . . . Retrieved July 30, 2015, from http://mentalhealthrecovery.com/wrap-is/

Depression. (2016). Retrieved March 20, 2016, from http://www.nami.org/Learn-More/Mental-Health-Conditions/Depression

Depression and Suicide Risk. (2014). Retrieved June 01, 2016, from http://www.suicidology. org/portals/14/docs/resources/factsheets/2011/ depressionsuicide2014.pdf

Depression Fact Sheet - NAMI: The National ... (2013). Retrieved July 27, 2015, from http:// www2.nami.org/factsheets/mentalillness_ factsheet.pdf

Dual Diagnosis. (2016). Retrieved March 3, 2016, from https://www.nami.org/Learn-More/ Mental-Health-Conditions/Related-Conditions/ Dual-Diagnosis

General Mental Health Facts. (n.d.). Retrieved June7, 2016, from http://www.nami.org/ NAMI/media/NAMI Media/Infographics/ GeneralMHFacts.pdf

Grella, C.E., Greenwell, L., Mays, V.M., & Cochran, S.D. (2009) *Influence of gender, sexual orientation, and need on treatment utilization for substance use and mental disorders: Findings from the California Quality of Life Survey*. BMC Psychiatry. 9:52.

Harvard Health Publications (2009) accessed from: http://www.health.harvard.edu/mind-and-mood/what-causes-depression

How Antidepressants Work: SSRIs, MAOIs, Tricyclics, and More. (2005-2016). Retrieved July 27, 2015, from http://www.webmd.com/depression/how-different-antidepressants-work

liar (2015). In *Merriam-Webster.com*. Retrieved July 27, 2015, from http://www.merriam-webster.com dictionary/liar

Link, B. G., & Phelan, J. C. (2001). *Conceptualizing Stigma*. Annu. Rev. Sociol. Annual Review of Sociology, 27(1), 363-385. doi:10.1146/annurev.soc.27.1.363

Mayo Clinic Staff, 2016 -1998-2016 Mayo Foundation for Medical Education and Research http://www.mayoclinic.org/diseases-conditions/depression/basics/definition/con-20032977

Mental Health By the Numbers. (2016). Retrieved August 5, 2015, from https://www. nami.org/Learn-More/Mental-Health-By-the-Numbers

Mental Illness FACTS AND NUMBERS - NAMI: The National ... (2013). Retrieved August 3, 2015, from http://www2.nami.org/factsheets/mentalillness_factsheet.pdf

moves (2015). In *Merriam-Webster.com*. Retrieved July 27, 2015, from http://www.merriam-webster.com/dictionary/moves

National Collaborating Centre for Mental Health (UK). Depression: The Treatment and Management of Depression in Adults (Updated Edition). Leicester (UK): British Psychological Society; 2010. (NICE Clinical Guidelines, No. 90.) Available from: http://www.ncbi.nlm.nih.gov/books/NBK63748/

National Institutes of Health (March, 2016).
NIH senior health: Built with you in mind.
Taking medicines: Drugs in the body. Retrieved
June 5, 2016 from http://nihseniorhealth.gov/
takingmedicines/drugsinthebody/01.html

National Institutes of Health (US); Biological
Sciences Curriculum Study. NIH Curriculum
Supplement Series [Internet]. Bethesda (MD):
National Institutes of Health (US); 2007.
Information about Mental Illness and the Brain.
Available from: http://www.ncbi.nlm.nih.gov/
books/NBK20369/

playbook (2015). In *Merriam-Webster.com*.
Retrieved July 27, 2015, from http://www.
merriam-webster.com/dictionary/playbook

Preamble to the Constitution of the World
Health Organization as adopted by the
International Health Conference, New York,
19-22 June, 1946; signed on 22 July 1946 by the
representatives of 61 States (Official Records of
the World Health Organization, no. 2, p. 100)
and entered into force on 7 April 1948.

Richey, C. (2014). *Cliff Richey: Don't face depression alone*. Posted on the San Angelo Standard Times website May 22, 2014. http://www.gosanangelo.com/news/dont-face-depression-alone

Richey, C. and Richey Kallendorf, H., Ph.D (2010). *Acing depression: a tennis champion's toughest match*. New Chapter Press.

Salters-Pedneault, K., Ph.D. (2015, January 15). What is Stigma? - HealthyPlace. Retrieved June 04, 2016, from http://www.healthyplace.com/stigma/stand-up-for-mental-health/what-is-stigma/

self-medicate (2007). *The American Heritage Medical Dictionary*. Retrieved June 7, 2016 from http://medical-dictionary.thefreedictionary.com/Self-medicating

stigma (2015). In *Merriam-Webster.com*. Retrieved July 27, 2015, from http://www.merriam-webster.com/dictionary/stigma

Stigma Fact Sheet - NAMI: The National ... (n.d.). Retrieved June 4, 2016, from http://www2. nami.org/factsheets/mentalillness_factsheet.pdf

Suicide FACT SHEET - NAMI: National Alliance on Mental Illness. (2015, March). Retrieved July 30, 2015, from http://www.nami.org/factsheets/ suicide_factsheet.pdf

Suicide in American: Frequently Asked Questions (2015). Science Writing, Press & Dissemination Branch (2015, April). Retrieved May 30, 2016, from http://www.nimh.nih.gov/ health/topics/suicide-prevention/index.shtml

teammates (2015). In *Merriam-Webster.com*. Retrieved July 27, 2015, from http://www. merriam-webster.com/dictionary/teammates

the ball is in your court (2015). In *Merriam-Webster.com*. Retrieved July 27, 2015, from http://www.merriam-webster.com/dictionary/ theballisinyourcourt

The Connection Between Mental Illness and Substance Abuse | Dual Diagnosis. (2016). Retrieved June 07, 2016, from http://www. dualdiagnosis.org/mental-health-and-addiction/ the-connection/

therapeutic dose (2012). *Farlex Partner Medical Dictionary*. Retrieved June 5, 2016 from http:// medicaldictionary.thefreedictionary.com/ therapeutic+dose

titration (2009). *Mosby's Medical Dictionary, 8th edition*. Retrieved June 5, 2016 from http:// medical-dictionary.thefreedictionary.com/ titration

U.S. DEPARTMENT OF HEALTH AND HUMAN SERVICES National Institutes of Health NIH Publication No. TR 13-3561 Revised 2013

U.S. Food and Drug Administration. (2009, January 9). Understanding Antidepressant Medications. Retrieved from http://www. fda.gov/forconsumers/consumerupdates/ ucm095980.htm#TypesofAntidepressants

World Psychiatry, 2002, Feb 1(1), p 16-20, Patrick Corrigan and Amy Watson: *Forum – stigma and mental illness: Understanding the impact of stigma on people with mental illness.*

Wyatt, R.C. and Seid, E.L. (2009). Instructor's Manual for COGNITIVE-BEHAVIORAL THERAPY with DONALD MEICHENBAUM, PHD from the series PSYCHOTHERAPY WITH THE EXPERTS. http://www.psychotherapy.net/ data/uploads/5110394f10a74.pdf

ALSO FROM
NEW CHAPTER PRESS

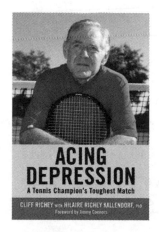

Acing Depression, A Tennis Champions Toughest Match
By Cliff Richey with Hillaire Richey Kallendorf, PhD

Chronicling the tumultuous life of the original bad boy of tennis, this engaging memoir describes one man's public battle with clinical depression. Describing torturous days in which he would place black trash bags on the windows and lay in bed crying for hours, this brutally honest narrative stresses that depression is a mental disorder that can affect anyone.

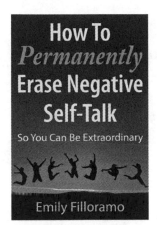

How to Permanently Erase Negative Self-Talk: So You Can Be Extraordinary Paperback

By Emily Filloramo

How To Permanently Erase Negative Self-Talk: So You Can Be Extraordinary teaches you how to access the real cause of your struggles—the negative messages imprinted on the subconscious since childhood—and heal the wounded parts of you that are holding onto the pain, misunderstandings, and gut-wrenching memories that prevent you from feeling good.

Macci Magic: Extracting Greatness From Yourself and Others

by Rick Macci with Jim Martz

Master coach Rick Macci shares his secrets to success both on and off the tennis court in this much-anticipated first book. Through anecdotes and more than 100 sayings that exemplify his teaching philosophy, this inspirational manual helps pave the way to great achievement not only in tennis, but in business and in life.

Lessons from the Wild

by Shayamal Vallabhjee

Simple yet powerful in its messages, this motivational guide draws inspiration from an inconspicuous group of wild animals. A heartwarming collection of factual stories is presented, drawing a parallel between the animals' struggles and the human race's daily challenges.

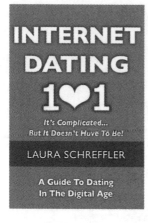

Internet Dating 101: It's Complicated...But It Doesn't Have To Be: The Digital Age Guide to Navigating Your Relationship Through Social Media and Online Dating Sites
by Laura Schreffler

An all-encompassing guide for those wanting to use social media to look for love in the digital age, Internet Dating 101: It's Complicated But It Doesn't Have to Be! is a humorous yet helpful book that navigates the ins and outs of Facebook, Twitter, online dating sites, e-mail and more.

The Greatest Tennis Matches of All Time

by Steve Flink

Author and tennis historian Steve Flink profiles and ranks the greatest tennis matches in the history of the sport. Roger Federer, Billie Jean King, Rafael Nadal, Bjorn Borg, John McEnroe, Martina Navratilova, Rod Laver, and Chris Evert are all featured in this book that breaks down, analyzes, and puts into historical context the most memorable matches ever played.